SELLING OUR YOUTH

Great Debates in Higher Education is a series of short, accessible books addressing key challenges to and issues in Higher Education, on a national and international level. These books are research informed but debate driven. They are intended to be relevant to a broad spectrum of researchers, students and administrators in higher education, and are designed to help us unpick and assess the state of higher education systems, policies, and social and economic impacts.

RECENTLY PUBLISHED IN THIS SERIES

Combatting Marginalisation by Co-Creating Education: Methods, Theories and Practices from the Perspectives of Young People
Edited by David Thore Gravesen, Kaz Stuart, Mette Bunting, Sidse Hølvig Mikkelsen and Peter Hornbæk Frostholm

Challenging the Teaching Excellence Framework: Diversity Deficits in Higher Education Evaluations
Amanda French and Kate Carruthers Thomas

Leadership of Historically Black Colleges and Universities: A what not to do Guide for HBCU Leaders
Johnny D. Jones

The Fully Functioning University
Tom Bourner, Asher Rospigliosi and Linda Heath

A Brief History of Credit in UK Higher Education: Laying Siege to the Ivory Tower
Wayne Turnbull

Degendering Leadership in Higher Education
Barret Katuna

Cultural Journeys in Higher Education: Student Voices and Narratives
Jan Bamford and Lucy Pollard

Perspectives on Access to Higher Education
Sam Broadhead, Rosemarie Davis and Anthony Hudson

Radicalisation and Counter-Radicalisation in Higher Education
Catherine McGlynn and Shaun McDaid

Refugees in Higher Education: Debate, Discourse and Practice
Jacqueline Stevenson and Sally Baker

The Marketisation of English Higher Education: A Policy Analysis of a Risk-Based System
Colin McCaig

Access to Success and Social Mobility through Higher Education: A Curate's Egg?
Edited by Stuart Billingham

Evaluating Scholarship and Research Impact: History, Practices, and Policy Development
Jeffrey W. Alstete, Nicholas J. Beutell, and John P. Meyer

Sexual Violence on Campus: Power-Conscious Approaches to Awareness, Prevention, and Response
Chris Linder

Higher Education, Access and Funding: The UK in International Perspective
Edited by Sheila Riddell, Sarah Minty, Elisabet Weedon, and Susan Whittaker

British Universities in the Brexit Moment: Political, Economic and Cultural Implications
Mike Finn

Teaching Excellence in Higher Education: Challenges, Changes and the Teaching Excellence Framework
Amanda French and Matt O'Leary

SELLING OUR YOUTH

Graduate Stories of Class, Gender and Work in Challenging Times

BY

HARRIET BRADLEY

University of the West of England, Bristol, UK

RICHARD WALLER

University of the West of England, Bristol, UK

And

LAURA BENTLEY

University of Birmingham, UK

United Kingdom – North America – Japan – India
Malaysia – China

Emerald Publishing Limited
Howard House, Wagon Lane, Bingley BD16 1WA, UK

First edition 2022

Reprints and permissions service
Contact: permissions@emeraldinsight.com

British Library Cataloguing in Publication Data
A catalogue record for this book is available from the British Library

ISBN: 978-1-80117-239-4 (Print)
ISBN: 978-1-80117-236-3 (Online)
ISBN: 978-1-80117-238-7 (Epub)

Printed and bound by CPI Group (UK) Ltd, Croydon, CR0 4YY

ISOQAR certified
Management System,
awarded to Emerald
for adherence to
Environmental
standard
ISO 14001:2004.

Certificate Number 1985
ISO 14001

INVESTOR IN PEOPLE

CONTENTS

ABOUT THE AUTHORS

Harriet Bradley is Professor Emerita at Bristol and West of England Universities and Fellow of the Academy of Social Science. Her many publications include *Fractured Identities*, *Gender and Power in the Workplace* and *Men's Work, Women's Work*. She has written and researched widely on inequalities of class, gender and ethnicity. The *Paired Peers* project, funded by the Leverhulme Trust, is the latest of many research projects she has headed. The first book jointly authored by the project team, *Higher Education, Social Class and Social Mobility*, was awarded a prize by the Society for Education Studies.

Richard Waller is Professor of Education and Social Justice at the University of the West of England, Bristol, where he has worked since 1995. Richard's research explores the intersection of education, social class and identity, and is driven by a social justice agenda. In addition to the *Paired Peers* project upon which many of his key publications are based, Richard has also recently completed projects on combatting gender-based violence in universities, and a retrospective analysis of the Aim Higher widening participation initiative of the early 2000s. He is currently researching the experiences and motivations of working-class young men in higher education.

Laura Bentley is an ESRC Postdoctoral Research Fellow in the School of Social Policy at the University of Birmingham. She is the principal investigator for the project *Still Jenny from the Block? Working-class women, higher education and social mobility in the COVID context*. Previously, Laura has worked on the *Paired Peers* project and the *Revisiting the Needs of Sutton Coldfield: Change and Future Requirements* project. She is a co-convenor of the British Sociological Association's Social Class Study Group and hosts the *Working-class Women's Writing Retreat* for academics and students.

ACKNOWLEDGEMENTS

We would like to acknowledge the Leverhulme Trust for its funding of the *Paired Peers* project, especially its faith in us providing the second tranche for the follow-up study. We also want to acknowledge the other members of the team who worked with us to generate the data used in this book: Ann-Marie Bathmaker, Tony Hoare, Nicola Ingram, Jessie Abrahams, Vanda Papafilippou, Jody Mellor, Phoebe Beedell and Mike Ward. We are very grateful to Bristol University and the University of the West of England for assisting with this research.

Special thanks are due to Jessie Abrahams for conducting the survey reported on in Chapter 7 and sharing its data.

Harriet Bradley would like to thank the Economic and Social Research Council for its funding for the *Winners and Losers* project, data from which are also referred to in the book: the team for this project also included Steve Fenton, Jackie West, Will Guy and Ranji Devadason.

We thank our families for their forbearance and support while we were writing this book: (especially Steve Gillen, Caroline Laybourn, Charlie Waller, Eddie Waller, Daniel Round, Ben Copley and Lisa Copley).

Finally, we owe a massive debt to the fantastic young adults who gave their time and thoughts to be interviewed for our projects. Thank you for giving us permission to tell your stories and use quotations from the interviews. We wish you all the very best for your lives in these challenging times.

INTRODUCTION

It's a long term investment getting a degree. It's such an important investment for getting a good job that you wouldn't otherwise have, and I think it's pretty essential.
(University College London student George Phillips, interviewed in 2012) Parr, C. (2012)

The transition from university into stable employment has never been easy. However, in the 1960s, when the oldest of this book's three authors was a student at Bristol University, a steady stream of students from working-class backgrounds who had done well at school passed through the Higher Education (HE) system and entered professional employment, building careers as academics, lawyers, accountants, politicians, in the media and in arts. These 'baby boomers' were able to maintain good careers until retirement when they received solid pensions.

The objective of this book is to show how, in the twenty-first century, the fortunes of HE entrants are increasingly shaped by their class backgrounds. So much has changed since the 1960s. The proportion of young people who enter HE has increased greatly; in 1960 it was just 5%. The New Labour Government in 1997 set a target of 50% participation rate by 2010, which was common across the European Union, of which Britain was then a member. It has become the normal expectation of children in middle-class families that university will be part of their life journey, and increasingly working-class parents too have aspirations for their sons and daughters to attend university. In a time of economic uncertainty, a degree is seen as a passport to better prospects, as the quotation from George demonstrates. Such aspirations are particularly strong among some of Britain's ethnic minority populations, such as British Asian and Chinese heritage people, who see qualifications as a defence against racial discrimination. In the words of one of the young adults whose stories feature in this book, 'we are a degree generation'. Yet this ambitious cohort of young people is entering HE and the graduate labour market in a time of turmoil and crisis: the world recession of 2008 and the austerity policies that followed; the imposition of crippling fees and student loans to replace the generous free tuition and maintenance grants of the post-war decades; the prevalence of insecure forms of employment; and finally in 2020 a world pandemic caused by coronavirus.

We draw in this book on the stories of young adults who were interviewed for a research project, *Paired Peers*, funded by the Leverhulme Trust. This unique project followed a group of undergraduates at Bristol's two universities from the start of their first year of study for a seven-year period. We started with a sample of 90 and at the end of the seventh year were still in touch with 56. They were interviewed up to 10 times each, so we have a detailed account from each of their experiences as students and as entrants to the labour market. In Chapter 2 of this book, we provide an introduction to our research, the city of Bristol and its two universities.

This book focuses on how the social class background of these students has shaped their experiences, both as students and as graduates. Class, of course, is a highly contested and sensitive issue. Moreover, as our societies have evolved and economies changed, the nature of class relations has changed, becoming more complex. We will indicate some of these complexities as we tell the stories of our young adult participants, and in Chapter 2 we will explain how we categorized our participants as either middle-class or working-class, based on a mix of factors.

Despite the debates around class, both social scientists and politicians assert that social mobility between classes is currently limited and that HE should provide a solution. Researchers Kate Purcell and Peter Elias, in an important paper on the impact of HE on equal opportunities, ask three questions:

1. Has university expansion enabled working-class students to get better jobs?

2. Has it allowed them to compete equally with middle-class peer students?

3. Does it provide means for those from advantaged backgrounds to succeed, thereby reinforcing the existing class order?

As they put it: 'the answer to the first question may be yes, but the answer to the second is no, and to the third a resounding yes' (Elias & Purcell, 2013, p. 20). As a result, they continue, though the number of students in HE has dramatically increased, the proportion from disadvantaged backgrounds has remained stable over the past 40 years, and they are increasingly having to enter non-graduate jobs when they graduate. This sad picture is confirmed in Diane Reay's wonderful book on education and inequality, *Miseducation* (2017). Reay draws upon decades of research carried out with schools, working-class young people, their parents and with university students, to show how the whole education system is stacked against working-class people's chances of success.

In Reay's studies, and in our own, use is made of the influential work of French social theorist, Pierre Bourdieu, especially his arguments that life chances are affected by the possession of, or lack of, certain types of resources or, as he called them, capitals. These are economic capital (possession of wealth, income and financial assets); social capital (access to networks of influential people) and cultural capital (knowledge, both academic and practical, and, particularly, familiarity with highly regarded forms of literature, music and the arts). A degree can itself be seen as educational capital, but to utilize that fully, the other forms of capital are needed: and, in general, middle-class families possess more valuable forms of all of them.

In Chapter 1 we draw on these studies and concepts to set the context for our own research, exploring the nature of contemporary labour markets and the position of graduates within them. We suggest that, as Guy Standing (2011) has argued, students and graduates may be in danger of entering the world of the 'precariat', a category of people defined by an insecure and transitory relationship to the world of work. Many of the *Paired Peers* participants found short-term employment in what is known as the 'gig economy'. Yet we argue that in relative terms it still pays to be a graduate, so Chapter 1 also briefly considers the experience of those young people who lack HE experience and are therefore even more vulnerable to economic insecurity. Recent research has shown that, while some young school leavers may earn better wages than graduates in their starter roles, in a few years' time graduate earnings outstrip non-graduate, what is known as the 'graduate premium' (Blanchflower, 2019).

The next set of Chapters, 3–6, look in detail at the experience of the graduates in our study, drawing on the rich narratives they offered us to build a picture of the character-istic pathways of four different groups: middle-class men, middle-class women, working-class men and working-class women. We show how their career pathways are strongly shaped by both class and gender, but also tease out some of the complexities of class within these broad groupings.

But, you may ask, does it matter? Are not these differences predictable and unavoidable? Our answer is that it does absolutely matter. All political parties profess concern about lack of social mobility in our society. A report from the Sutton Trust (2019) showed how elite professions are filled with people who went to private schools and thence to prestigious universities. For example, while in 2016 only 7% of the population attended independent schools, 74% of judges, 61% of senior doctors, 71% of top military officers and 51% of journalists were privately educated. Moreover, these top people are disproportionately drawn from Oxford and Cam-bridge Universities (Oxbridge): 74% of the judiciary, 54% of leading journalists and 47% of the MPs in the Conservative cabinet. Perhaps even more shockingly, in the Labour shadow cabinet, 32% went to Oxbridge: this is the party founded to represent the interests of working-class people. As Owen Jones' book on the elite, *The Establishment; and how they get away with it* (2014), also confirms, these senior people are the decision-makers and law-givers in our society, but have little experience and understanding of the lives and views of ordi-nary working people. Consequently, they tend to govern in the interests of their own class and reflect its values and morality. Jones' other well-known book, *Chavs* (2011), reveals how increasingly rather than being seen as 'the salt of the earth' as they were in the post-war period, British working-people are despised and looked down on, stereotyped as lazy losers and scroungers; more like, as Jones put it, 'the scum of the earth'. As a highly offensive but not untypical example, in January

2021 a Conservative local party chairman, Dr Gareth Baines, was forced to resign after tweeting that hospital Accident and Emergency departments were 'full of fat mums in pot-noodle-stained leggings/pjs taking their kids for a day out at A&E to harvest Facebook likes, because their darling little snot-covered ASBO fell over' (Mail Online, 10 Jan 2021).

Thus, the final chapter of the book will consider what can be done to contest these patterns of privilege and disadvantage. What policies should be adopted by schools, universities, employers and politicians if we are sincere in wanting to create a more just and equal society? Or are we happy to accept educational and economic conditions which lead, as we shall show, to mental stress and depression in a generation of young people, resigned to 'selling our youth', in the words of one young graduate in our study, in an exploitative and precarious global marketplace?

1

YOUNG GRADUATES' EMPLOYMENT TRAJECTORIES IN CONTEXT

The young women and men whose stories are told in subsequent chapters in this book belong to what is known as 'Generation Y' or 'Gen Y', those who were born between 1981 and 1996. They are also often known as 'millennials' as they grew up around the millennium. Unfortunately for them, they were growing to adulthood when the recession of 2008 struck, with devastating effects on the future economy. Here in the United Kingdom, the Conservative Government led by David Cameron and George Osborne responded to this crisis with austerity policies, drastically cutting back public spending. These policies led to rising unemployment and debt, and in 2011 involved significant increasing of fees for attending a higher education institution (HEI) from £3,290 to a ceiling of £9,000 (Govt. policy briefing document: https://researchbriefings.files.parliament.uk/documents/SN05753/SN05753.pdf). Although during the election of 2010 the Liberal Democratic Party, along with the Labour Party, promised to remove fees, when the Lib Dems led by Nick

Clegg entered into coalition with the Conservatives, they reneged on that pledge. As a result the young millennials who entered university faced taking out loans which would leave them with large amounts of debt on graduation.

Because of these impacts of recession and austerity, Generation Y, and their successors, Generation Z, are considered to be the first generations in the modern era who will be worse off than their parents. They have been popularly referred to as *Generation Crunch* (after the so-called credit crunch), *Generation Rent* (because of their inability to purchase accommodation) and *The Lost Generation* (because of the limiting of employment options). Howker and Malik (2013) wrote a useful book about the plight of Gen Y, entitled *Jilted Generation*; they argued that older people's greed was depriving young people of chances to achieve a decent lifestyle. This idea was also developed by former Conservative Higher Education (HE) minister, David Willetts, whose book was provocatively titled *The Pinch: How the baby boomers took their children's future and why they should give it back* (2010). Similar ideas were expressed in the United States by Bruce Cannon Gibney and can be found in a series of YouTube clips. Across Europe the same phenomenon was observed and various labels were given to Gen Y and Gen Z.

This chapter sets the scene, discussing the difficult economic context in which the young adults' stories we will highlight were played out. Then we briefly review previous studies exploring the situation of young graduates: as they are still considered to do better than their contemporaries who have not entered HE, we give some details of the issues non-graduates may face in education and employment. Next we address the thorny and contested issue of how to define social class in contemporary Britain. Finally, since we espouse an intersectional approach to understanding inequalities, we discuss particular disadvantages related to gender and ethnicity impacting on young people's lives.

LABOUR MARKETS IN RECESSION

It is important to stress that the phenomenon of graduate underemployment or unemployment is not entirely new. Entering one's first job is a difficult business and young entrants' trajectories have long been marked by 'churn', that is shifting between various different jobs before settling into an occupation. Back in 1985, the *Guardian* newspaper featured the story of Heather, who at 21, after dropping out of university where she was studying Economics, had failed to get any kind of job and was stuck on the dole. Describing herself as dwelling in 'one of the nation's unemployment blackspots', she explained she had to live with her parents, which, as we will see, is a familiar contemporary pattern.

Heather and her classmates all stayed on at school until they had secured a job or a university place. Until recently that was the expectation of most school-leavers. As part of a project, *Winners and Losers* (see Acknowledgements), studying young adults' employment histories in 2000, a research team from the University of Bristol visited schools and colleges. A careers adviser at one college reported the high aspirations typically held by the students: 'they all say they don't want a boring nine to five job, they want a job where they are travelling, meeting people…they have a perception that if they do a degree they are going to get this really whizzy job where they are chairing board meetings and doing presentations'. Young women at an elite girls' private school confirmed that view. One told the researcher 'Everyone thinks I'm going to get a job that's highly paid and I'm going to get rich'. Another commented cynically 'We're all highly trained, they've got us going to universities and colleges and becoming accountants'. Their teacher commented wryly that most pupils were focused on money and a consumerist lifestyle, presumably influenced by the experiences of well-off parents.

The adviser offered a more realistic vision, encouraging them to see their career 'not as a well-made road, but as crazy paving which you have to lay yourself'. She was correct, because, even in the relatively prosperous years before what David Blanchflower (2019) calls the 'Great Recession' of 2007–2008, there was talk of the end of 'a job for life'. Young people were being warned they would have to adapt and acquire skills to steer them through 'fractured transitions' (Bradley & Devadason, 2008; Furlong & Cartmel, 2007; Roberts, 1995).

Young people's visions of the future, however, were clearly shaped by class. While the young middle-class people referred to above conceptualized their futures in terms of careers, working-class youths were more likely to talk of jobs. David, a careers coordinator at a school in a deprived working-class area of Bristol, told us the young people's aspirations were to 'have a nice house, have children and a job which pays reasonably well'. This supported other research from that period: for example, these were the ambitions of young working-class men studied in Cambridge by Linda McDowell (2003).

David believed these students had realistic hopes for employment, the boys considering mechanical trades and the girls childcare, nursery and primary school teaching. Many of these pupils had 'Saturday jobs' at Cribbs Causeway, a huge shopping mall on the outskirts of Bristol. Working in retail and catering, they considered gaining jobs there full-time. In contrast to middle-class pupils who might travel away to attend university, these youngsters were deeply rooted in their

Bristol communities, expecting to stay there. David told us of two young men who went to Reading to enlist in the army, but missed their family, friends and girlfriends so much that they quit and returned to Bristol.

The pattern reported by David, careers for the middle-class, jobs for the working-class, was one that had evolved since the war, and was described classically in Ashton and Field's *Young Worker* study (1975). They distinguished three typical pathways for the transition from school to work. Middle-class pupils progressed to university or polytechnic and went into professional employment. Working-class students left at the earliest leaving age and went into 'unskilled' work (for example, factory or retail); and a middle group, consisting of some working-class and some lower-middle class youths, attended sixth form or college, taking up apprenticeships, or entering clerical work such as banking, or intermediate careers such as nursing.

This pattern of classed transitions had, however, begun to fray by the time of the *Winners and Losers* study, reflecting the changes that had occurred since the 1980s to the British economy. Production of goods and services had been subject to an increasing process of globalization, meaning that, for example, car parts produced in one country could be assembled in another. This trend encouraged companies to move aspects of production from the rich nations of the Global North to poorer, less developed countries where labour was cheaper: a classic example was the removal of call centres from Britain to India. Such change led to mass unemployment and downward pressure on manual wages, what has been called 'a race to the bottom' (Joliffe & Collins, 2019). It also hastened the ongoing process of deindustrialization in Britain: the steady decline of manufacturing and primary production, with jobs in the service sector becoming numerically dominant. Thus, men who had worked in the traditional heavy industries such as mining and steel were either forced to take lower-paid, less secure jobs, in sectors like retail, care or security, or else become unemployed. What became known as 'the crisis of masculinity' ensued, as men increasingly felt unsure about their roles and identities (Ingram & Waller, 2014; McInnes, 1998).

These changes were augmented by changes in economic policy instituted in the 1980s by the Thatcher Government, and carried on by subsequent regimes. The most notable feature was privatization of many nationalized industries (railways, gas, water and electricity) and of services provided by the state (from prison facilities to school meal provision). Privatization of public services was notably increased, decades later after the recession of 2008, as Conservative leaders Cameron and Osborne responded by imposing a regime of austerity. Cuts to local government funding led to the loss of many well-paid secure council posts and their replacement by subcontracted jobs, often with poor pay, and inferior conditions. Secure work gave way to temporary 'project work' and short-term contracts. Such conditions were experienced by many of the young graduates in the *Paired Peers* research, who, having expected that their degrees would lead to well-paid professional work, found themselves forced into low-wage low-skilled jobs.

Accordingly the young generations of the twenty-first century have found themselves grappling with adverse economic conditions and decreasing opportunities. These trends had started to appear at the start of the century. The *Winners and Losers* project found that young adults did not expect a job for life, were often low-paid and were not settling into a steady job or career until their 30s (Bradley & Devadason, 2008). Many other youth researchers noted how transitions from school to work were being lengthened and that increasingly young people were moving in and out of statuses – full-time work, education and training, temporary work, unemploy-ment, some even forced into 'fiddly jobs' in the black economy (see for example, Furlong & Cartmel, 2007; McDonald 2005; Roberts, 1995).

All the processes described above were ramped up as a result of the 2008 recession. A decade of austerity has led to downward pressures on wages and reduced prospects for the unfortunate young people of Gen Y and Gen X, including graduates, who have struggled in a hypercompetitive labour market to find rewarding employment. The *FutureTrack* quantitative study of Purcell et al. (2013) revealed that only a minority of graduates will attain traditional graduate jobs in fields like law, media or academia. Some will find their way into newer areas of the economy which Purcell et al. (2013) call 'new graduate jobs', such as event management and web design, but others will end up in non-graduate areas, such as retail and bar work. Blanchflower sums it up succinctly in relation to similar processes in America:

> *College graduates take jobs previously done by high school graduates, who have to take jobs previously done by high school dropouts, who struggle to find work.*

(Blanchflower, 2019, p. 5)

A race to the bottom indeed!

Two fairly recent contractual changes have particularly affected the young graduates in our study, *the gig economy* and *zero-hours contracts*. Both these are devices enabling employers to cut costs and lessen their tax burden. The 'gig economy' refers to a labour market sector in which people are employed on short-term contracts or as freelancers. The name is taken from the entertainment world where musicians and other performers are hired for a particular event or tour, a 'gig'; workers are not given a regular wage but are paid for specific tasks, such as a food delivery. Well-known examples of gig employers are Uber, the taxi hire firm, and Deliveroo, a food delivery company: students are a favoured form of worker for this service. Another example is the hiring of numbers of law graduates by banks and finance companies to work as paralegals on a time-limited project for a client. Workers in the gig economy lack legal protection and job security, can be fired without notice and may lack entitlement to paid holidays or sick pay. Similarly, zero-hours contracts are a form of insecure employment: workers are hired without any set time-frame, so the employer can change the number of working hours at will to suit demand. Zero-hours contracts are common in retail, care work and leisure. They afford little security, although court cases have ruled that if the workers are continuously employed they may claim holiday pay, but not sick pay. It is estimated that five million people were in the gig economy in 2019, while the Labour Force Survey in that year reported 896,000 workers on zero-hours contracts (ONS, 2019).

For some people, including undergraduate and post-graduate students, these irregular working arrangements may offer a degree of flexibility and freedom, as they can be fitted around their studies. However, the unpredictability of 'gigs' or hours means that workers are unable to anticipate their likely earnings from week to week. For that reason they can be seen as part of the global phenomenon of the *precariat* as defined by Guy Standing, a concept which will be discussed in the next section.

GRADUATE STRUGGLES IN THE POST-RECESSION SOCIETY

To increase young people's woes, this same period has been marked by a housing market in which house prices have been spiralling upward continually, a trend which accelerated during the global coronavirus pandemic. This is matched by ever-increasing rents in a private sector dominated by voracious developers and landlords, profiting from the 'buy to let' system. Not only is Britain marked by its excessive embracing of the principles of globalization and the neoliberal free market, it has also enthusiastically adopted rentier capitalism: conventional wisdom highlighted property as a safer investment than stocks and shares after the stock exchange and banking crashes. As we shall see, the majority of prestigious graduate jobs are in London, but the costs of renting are so high that only those from wealthy backgrounds or attaining top jobs can afford them. Consequently, many graduates have to return to their home areas to find affordable accommodation and perhaps to 'boomerang' back to live with their parents. The proportion of young adults living in the parental home has been steadily rising over past decades. Many of the graduates in our study have had spells back at home, some of them prolonged. Moreover, the prospects of owning a home seem remote or unobtainable for many. Only where two people have a good salary is a mortgage affordable or where rich parents can buy their children a flat or town house. Bristol, too, is characterized by expensive housing, though rents and house prices are somewhat lower than London.

Add to this, graduates carry a burden of debt out of university. Although repayments do not commence until a certain income level is reached (£18,000 for *Paired Peers* graduates), this is likely to be the time when they earn enough to consider a mortgage. In this respect, however, our cohort was luckier than the students who followed them, since fees then were £3,290 a year; shortly they would rise to £9,000. Some participants from less wealthy backgrounds told us that this increase would have deterred them from attending university or at least made them choose a more vocational degree with enhanced employment opportunities.

The issue of housing affordability is a crucial one because leaving the parental home is seen as a marker of becoming independent and attaining adulthood. Sociologists of youth, such as Gill Jones (2005) and Bob Coles (1995), have argued that youth transitions should be seen as threefold: the transition from education into work, the transition into independent living and the establishing of a new family of one's own outside the family of origin. These three combine to mark the maturation into full adulthood. However, since the 1980s increased youth unemployment along with extended proportions staying into further and higher education has brought what Hollands (1997) called 'The Long Transition' making this process not just longer but more complex:

> *During the course of barely half a century, the steps that are central to the transition – leaving school, starting a working career, leaving home, founding a family – have become less synchronized…As a consequence the status of young people in society has become more ambiguous: in some respects they are treated as adults, in others they remain dependent on their families and/or on state contributions.*
> (Bradley & Van Hoof, 2005, p. 3)

Part of the cause of this lengthened transition has been the greater proportion of young people entering higher education. In autumn 2021, 38% of the UK's population aged 18 embarked on a university degree, the highest percentage on record (UCAS, 2021). This is a 17% increase on numbers admitted five years previously. Antonucci (2016) found 32% of her sample of students came from manual and technical occupations: 47% were first in their family to attend university. As stated earlier, HE has become the norm for young people from middle-class families and is increasingly popular for working-class youths from more aspirational families:

> *I was always going to go to university. It wasn't a question of not...both my parents went to university and everyone from my school went to university.*
> (Elliot, middle-class, UoB)

In view of the 'race for the bottom', it is a rational decision to seek qualifications to improve your chances of getting a good job. Unfortunately, as studies by Phillip Brown and colleagues have shown, the search for good jobs has become highly competitive with the supply of graduates outrunning demand (Brown & Tannock, 2009). This is partly due to what Brown et al. (2011) call 'the global auction for talent'. The freeing up of the movement of people around the world attendant on globalization allows employers to seek out those they consider the most talented applicants from different countries. This is particularly the case in the finance industry, but also is marked in engineering, academia and medicine. To gain 'top jobs', as we shall see, graduates have to indulge in a complex game of acquiring assets to demonstrate 'talent', both in terms of educational capital (good degrees from top universities) and showing personal resourcefulness in clocking up extra-curricular achievements and demonstrating abstract 'soft skills' (Bathmaker et al., 2013).

It matters greatly what university you attend, not just in terms of the opportunities open to you but the salary you can earn. In 2016 the government published its first findings from the Longitudinal Education Outcomes survey, an analysis of the median earnings of law graduates five years after gradu-ating in 2008–2009. They found that law graduates from Oxford earned £61,000 contrasted with the University of Bradford graduates on £17,000: the gap is enormous. Unsurprisingly the top 10 institutions with highest-paid law graduates were all elite Russell Group (RG) universities (including Bristol University on £37,000), while the bottom 10 were all 'new universities' which had been polytechnics or colleges of HE before 1992. The so-called 'Golden Triangle' of Oxford, Cambridge and London headed the table (*Times Higher* 8 December 2016). No surprise that so many of our MPs and judges attend these elite HEIs.

These were the prevailing conditions when our graduate cohort left the University of Bristol (UoB) and the University of the West of England (UWE) in 2013 to set out on their journey into employment. However, things have become even grimmer in the recent period with the advent of the corona-virus and its impact on the economy. In November 2020 the *Sunday Times* ran an article on the plight of recent graduates. They cited the case of a Southampton University graduate with a Master's in Civil Engineering: having applied for over 70 jobs, she secured only one interview. Forced to move back to live with her parents and sign up for universal credit she described her situation as 'draining, stressful and frustrating' (Kelly, 2020). The case is the more shocking as Engineering is seen as a discipline offering strong employment opportunities.

The TUC reported that over the summer of 2020 young workers under 25 fared worse than other age groups, with 59,000 losing jobs between July and September. From the onset of COVID, university graduates constituted almost a third of new Universal Credit claimants (32%, compared to 26% previously), with even greater increase for 'younger' graduates aged 18–39 (41%, compared to 28% previously)

(Edmiston et al., 2020). Young people tend to be concentrated in leisure, hospitality and retail, sectors badly affected by lockdowns. As we shall discuss later, the prospects of those who have not attended university are the worst, but graduates may also struggle.

Indeed, many new graduates can be viewed as being in danger of becoming what Guy Standing (2011) calls the 'precariat'. Standing uses this term to describe what he sees as a new class emerging as a result of globalization and neoliberalism. This class is distinct by virtue of its insecure and fractured relation to the labour market: employed in short-term jobs with poor contracts. Its members are in constant danger of falling into unemployment and thence into poverty. This is exacerbated by the confinement of many graduates to the rented housing sector. When an employment contract ends, under current benefit arrangements there will be a delay before Universal Credit payments can be accessed, leading to an inability to pay bills and the possibility of eviction. This is what drives many young adults to return to the parental home.

The presence of highly qualified people among the precariat is one factor distinguishing it from the working-class, or 'proletariat', as Karl Marx called it. Another is that while work gave traditional working-class people an identity – a miner, a cook, a factory worker – and thus a frame around which to create a life narrative and perhaps a sense of community, those in the precariat lack a shaping identity from their occupation because of their episodic and fractured engagement with employment.

This argument chimes with the highly influential work of Ulrich Beck who argued that from the middle of the twentieth century there evolved what he called *reflexive modernity*, a phase of social development in which people become more aware of their ability to make free choices about the direction

of their life. Central to this was the idea that class forms of
social and cultural identity had given way to *individualization*
(Beck & Beck-Gernsheim, 2001): instead of accepting one's
social situation as a given (one was born a peasant, a worker,
an aristocrat), people were increasingly required to construct
their own identity and take responsibility for the circumstances of their life. This idea lies behind a lot of current
political thinking, whereby, for example, the poor are deemed
to suffer poverty because of their personal failures, making
bad choices or being lazy (Jones, 2011). While such ideas have
emanated from middle-class politics, an interesting piece by
Sarah Evans shows how sections of the working-class have
adopted this perspective (2010). Evans studied a group of
working-class female college students and argued that they
viewed HE primarily as a means to 'becoming somebody',
making something of themselves:

> *The women with whom I spoke were highly
> motivated and looked forward to the identity that
> participating in the adult world of work would bring
> them. They often envisaged higher education in
> instrumental terms as a means of acquiring the
> capital to embark on the career pathway of their
> choice and all imagined themselves into middle-class,
> professional (and often traditionally masculine)
> careers in medicine, dentistry, law.*

(p. 61)

Ironically these aspirations for upward mobility were
combined with an acceptance of what Sennett has called 'the
hidden injuries of class' (Sennett & Cobb, 1977). Visiting
Cambridge, these young people experienced that university as
somewhere 'foreign' (Evans, 2010) where they would not fit.

Most intended to attend a local university and live at home (a typical working-class strategy).

Standing's (2011) idea of the precariat asserts the continuing salience of class. He identified three groups or fractions within the precariat. First, people who have fallen out of the old working class into precarity; second, migrants, refugees and members of minorities marginalized by majority populations. The third he named 'progressives', which would include some of our graduates; young people who go to university since they've been told this will give them a career and a secure future. The reality upon graduation is that they have no career, little in the way of future prospects, and plenty of debt.

Given all these circumstances, it is not surprising if throughout the last few decades anxiety and depression have been steadily rising among young people. There has been much attention to mental ill health among students, both undergraduate and postgraduate, which universities have seen as reaching crisis levels. Both UWE and UoB have launched major programmes to promote student well-being. The causes of distress include pressures to succeed in a climate of individualistic striving and awareness of the highly competitive jobs world, alongside some of the more destructive elements of student life and culture, such as poor housing, financial stress and overconsumption of alcohol and drugs and other risky behaviours, self-harming and even suicide (Waller et al., 2018). Some of this has impacted on some of our graduates; but at the same time, we are struck by the resourcefulness and creativity used by these young adults in finding their way through this demanding environment to make something of their lives.

MILLENNIALS AND CLASS IN HIGHER EDUCATION

The previous discussion has highlighted both the heightened supply of graduates, as a result of policies pushing university attendance as a route to occupational success, but also the over-supply identified in the research of Brown and others, causing massive competition for well-rewarded graduate jobs. While this may be an issue for all new graduates, the costs are likely to fall most heavily on those from working-class backgrounds. With fewer capital resources, they will find it more difficult to take the steps needed to win out in the competition. This was the issue explored with our *Paired Peers* participants, and it will be elaborated in subsequent chapters through the stories they told us. However, other researchers have studied the impact of class on university experiences and outcomes, and here we review a few key contributions.

Particularly notable is the work of Diane Reay, who has spent many decades studying the impact of class both within schools and in HE. Her findings are summarized in her useful text *Miseducation: inequality, education and the working-class* (2017) which tracks the fortunes of working-class youth through schools and into universities. Reay shows how working-class children attend the less well-resourced schools and are constructed within the system as deficient, because, as she summarizes it:

> *The working-class continue to have access to relatively low levels of the kind of material, cultural and psychological resources that aid educational success. Most cannot afford the private tuition and the enriching cultural activities that many upper- and*

> *middle-class parents routinely invest in for their*
> *children.*

(p. 15)

Research into middle-class parents, for example, by Devine (2004) and Lareau (2003) shows how vitally important their children's educational success is to them. They support school learning with their own involvement, helping with homework and buying educational materials (practices which sometimes continue into HE). The coronavirus pandemic exposed the fact that many poorer families, especially from ethnic minority communities, lacked not only computers and broadband but also basic materials such as pens, crayons and paper. If a middle-class child is seen to be failing at a state school, some parents will pay for a move into a private school; and Reay demonstrates how private tuition has become normal, even at primary school. In one predominantly middle-class school she studied, 65% of 11-year-olds were being tutored, with parents paying up to £100 per week. Reay notes how, deprived of such assets, working-class children suffered psychologically, internalizing ideas of themselves as 'thick' and attending 'rubbish schools'. Not surprising, then, that a UNICEF report in 2007 found that only 20% of UK children liked their school a lot.

Although there has been a steady increase of young working-class people overcoming these disadvantages to enter HE, simultaneously the system has become more stratified, with working-class students tending to attend less prestigious universities. For example, Reay notes that in 2013 only one in 20 of those enrolled in the elite RG universities had working-class backgrounds. Of children receiving free school meals (the poorest group) only 0.9% attended RG universities.

Privately educated children are much more likely to gain RG places, especially at Oxford and Cambridge.

Once at university, working-class students may find it harder to fit in and socialize with their middle-class peers, especially those making it to an RG institution (Bathmaker et al., 2016). In Reay's term, they are 'Strangers in Paradise' (Reay et al., 2009). While middle-class children learn from their schools, parents and older siblings about university life, those who are the first in their families to enter HE have no such knowledge. In the striking image used by Pierre Bourdieu and his followers, they are like 'a fish out of water' gasping to survive, while the middle-class students glide easily within currents. As Reay points out, they do not know the 'rules of the game' which will bring success, and this is exacerbated by financial pressures. They are more likely to struggle with rents and bills (leading many to choose universities near home, so they can stay with parents, as several of the working-class students in Chapters 5 and 6 did); more likely to take on term-time employment to survive and less likely to have the time or money to take part in extra-curricular activities to make their *curriculum vitae* (CV) look impressive to future employers (see also, Bathmaker et al., 2016). Reay notes that, on leaving university, graduates from the poorest 40% of families carry average debts of £57,000 compared to £43,000 for those from the richest 30%, while being more likely to earn less or be unemployed.

Reay's arguments are confirmed in a recent study by Ciaran Burke (2016), who carried out informative research on graduates in Northern Ireland. He conducted biographical interviews with 27 employed graduates, focusing on their educational histories, their family backgrounds and their post-graduation employment experiences. Burke argues that their trajectories were strongly shaped by their class backgrounds. Young middle-class people possessed more valuable forms of capital (social, economic and cultural, as outlined in the Introduction) than their working-class peers and were better able to 'play the game' of success in education and occupation.

Burke distinguished five groups among his graduate sample: strategic middle-class, strategic working-class, converted working-class, stalled middle-class and static working-class, the latter two groups being at time of interview in what Purcell and Elias describe as non-graduate jobs. The strategic middle-class were the winners in the graduate game: they understood what was necessary to get into university, were confident and at ease at school. Their parents were able to offer them guidance and financial support, and they developed successful strategies for obtaining well-paying sought-after jobs. The strategic working-class by contrast were less confident and knowledgeable about the education system and tended only gradually to develop strategies to get graduate jobs. Indeed, Burke argues that it was often only contact with more knowledgeable players which enabled them to secure professional work. The converted working-class were even less confident of their abilities, until some stroke of fortune (conversion) helped them towards success. Although Burke does not discuss it, the notion of 'luck' was commonly used by some of our participants to explain how they accessed jobs. Burke distinguished his fourth group, of two middle-class graduates, as being hyper-aspirational, based on over-confidence of their own ability, leading them to pursue unrealistic goals (acting, writing novels). Our study included some like these. The largest group were working-class students ending in non-graduate work: this cluster, sadly, were often lacking in self-confidence and clarity; they might have been pushed into applying to university by school or parents, and some had limited understanding of the 'rules of the game'.

For those determined working-class students who navigate their way through the obstacles they face both within university and in the transition to the labour market, there is yet another blockage they must face, what Friedman and Lauriston (2019) call 'the class ceiling'. Friedman and Lauriston carried out case studies in four prestigious occupations (media, accountancy, architecture and acting). They found that working-class entrants were blocked from promotion to top jobs and the highest pay. They noted a number of factors, including family support, informal sponsorship and, perhaps most significantly, fitting in. This involved what they describe as 'embodied capital', a type of self-presentation involving self-confidence, dress, deportment and speech, what the accountancy firm they studied called 'polish'. Linked to this was the practice of 'homophily', that is, the tendency of recruiters and promoters to select candidates similar to themselves, a practice that also discriminates against women (McDowell, 1996) and ethnic minorities. The resulting pay gap is highlighted in a study of the impact of private schooling by Green and Kynaston (2019) who report as follows:

> A *privately educated man (but not woman) leaving university with exactly the same degree as a state-educated man will later enjoy a pay gap of some 7–15% in his favour.*
>
> (p. 13)

They also note that privately educated men tend to gravitate to the highly rewarded financial services, especially in the City of London.

These studies focus on the obstacles to success of those from working-class backgrounds. However, another recent study by Antonucci (2016) highlights that the impact of the current economic constraints is not confined to this grouping.

Antonucci (2016), who interviewed students in England, Sweden and Italy, found that:

> *Disadvantage in HE is not only experienced by young people from lower socioeconomic backgrounds, but also from those of intermediate backgrounds (young people from the so-called 'squeezed middle').*

(p. x)

Antonucci argues that both groups share material hardships, such as living in substandard housing with impacts on their health and well-being, or lack of money, which forces them into prolonged semi-dependence on families who themselves struggle with limited resources. These circumstances may lead to mental health problems. We will see examples of this in the stories in subsequent chapters.

CLASS IN THE TWENTY-FIRST CENTURY

Antonucci's observation points to something that will be flagged up throughout this study, the complexity and ambiguities of social class. Previous studies have highlighted the major division between the two clusters we refer to as 'working-class' and 'middle-class', or what Bourdieusians label the dominated and dominant classes (Atkinson, 2010). Here, though, we wish to highlight the divisions *within* these two groupings: class fractions, as sociologists call them. For example, there are major differences within the middle-class in terms of possession of economic, social and cultural capital, between top professionals such as doctors and lawyers and those in intermediate occupations including nurses and clerical workers.

In the United Kingdom class is usually understood in occupational terms, which is how it is measured in official statistics. However, this is unsatisfactory, since many people do not have an occupation: children, pensioners, the unemployed, housewives, the chronically sick and, of course, university students. Yet all these people are still deeply embedded in the relations of class. It is better, then, to see class in broader terms:

> *A nexus of unequal lived relationships...These include the allocation of tasks in the division of labour (occupation, employment hierarchies); control and ownership within production; the unequal distribution of surplus (wealth, income, state benefits); patterns of consumption (lifestyle, living arrangements) and distinctive cultures that arise from all these (behavioural practices, community relations).*
>
> (Bradley, 2016, p. 70)

Someone's occupation is only one measure of their position in this web of relationships.

Moreover, class relations are highly dynamic, what Erickson and Goldthorpe (1992) called *The Constant Flux*. Class has its basis in economic relations, changing and developing with them. In the United Kingdom since the mid-twentieth century, the steady decline of manufacturing has led to a breaking up of long-established class communities, such as the mining villages of the North East or the factory towns of Lancashire. People who were made redundant found new employment, women as workers in the expanding consumerist industries (hospitality and beauty, for example) and males as 'white van men' offering construction services or deliveries. These processes of decomposition and re-composition of class continue as our economies evolve; the full impact of the coronavirus pandemic and its lockdowns have yet to be felt, but will be considerable as many businesses have closed down.

Despite these processes of change, there are senses in which the relations of class remain rooted, because, as emphasized in the definition above, class is lived within communities, where people share the same lifestyles, values and experiences. Koch et al. (2021) studied four towns, showing not only how strongly they displayed polarization between rich and poor areas but also how within those areas a sense of common feeling and solidarity was strong. Such community values were notably in display during the coronavirus pandemic, through street gatherings and singalongs, mutual aid groups and delivery services for those shielding, as people supported and engaged with their neighbours. These community bonds can act both as a resource and a trap, providing what American academic Robert Putnam (2000) has called bridging and bonding capital: bonding capital supports people 'getting by' but bridging helps in 'getting ahead'.

In this book we stress the divisions within each class. An analysis of the Norwegian elite by Toft and Friedman (2021) sets out a useful set of categories for exploring class. They distinguish between upper class (the elite), upper middle, lower middle, skilled working, unskilled working and primary groupings (forestry, agriculture and fishing). Beyond that, though, they divide the upper and middle classes into three groupings: those defined by cultural capital, those defined by economic capital and those with a balance of each. For example, the cultural upper middle class includes teachers, lecturers, journalists, artists; the balanced includes engineers, technicians and IT specialists, and the economic grouping contains managers, finance workers and business professionals.

There are, of course, alternative ways of conceptualizing class, but we hope what we outlined above will tally with the stories we are going to tell. While class relations in the twentieth century are more subtle, complex and changeable, they remain all-pervasive and mark our lives as individuals. This is particularly the case for youths who do not attend HE.

YOUTH AND EXCLUSION

Young people who lack education and training (often referred to as NEETS, not in education, employment or training) confront the harshest employment prospects (Antonucci, 2016). They are more likely to be low-paid in unrewarding jobs and to face spells of unemployment, sometimes prolonged. Unemployment often involves whole families, in areas where manufacturing has been in the greatest decline, including the valleys of South Wales, the North-East mining areas or Clydeside docklands. Struggling to survive on benefits, youths may turn to crime, to the drugs culture, while some end up homeless and sleeping in shop doorways or 'sofa surfing', staying temporarily with a series of friends.

Lowly-qualified young men and young women face different employment options, reflecting the fact that manual work and unskilled labour are more sex-segregated than professional and white-collar work. Girls may find work in hospitality, retail, hairdressing and care work, jobs built on skills they have learned in their home life. Beverley Skeggs (1997) studied young care workers and discovered the importance they placed on the value of *respectability* acquired through their jobs which distinguished them from the unemployed and benefit claimants. Skeggs argued this amounted to a 'misidentification' or denial of their class situation, marking them out from those they saw as 'beneath them', the poor. However, such care jobs, though plentiful, are low-paid and exhausting.

Nevertheless, things are better for these women than for their young male counterparts. The decline of factory work and especially of heavy industry (coal, steel, shipbuilding) meant jobs became limited: there is unskilled work in the construction industry and other labouring work, bar work, while some may find a job as a kind of informal apprentice to a self-employed craftsman. They may reluctantly enter female specialities, such as retail and care. The decline of the traditional apprenticeship schemes, which offered a major route of labour market entry for boys in the past, has closed doors for young hopefuls.

Case studies show how limited job opportunities may be and how they are strongly affected by location. Jobs are particularly limited in rural areas and small towns. Aniela Wenham (2020) studied young people in a seaside town in Yorkshire. She reports that disadvantaged young people in coastal towns are half as likely to gain two or more A-levels and to enter university compared to young people in major UK cities. Those she interviewed had left school with limited if any qualifications. Jobs were linked to the tourist industry, as one young man explained:

> Young people's work, it's normally waiting on holiday parks, you've only got like six holiday parks and they only have so many positions…Or you go to an agency, you get a zero-hour contract where you're not guaranteed any work.

Such youths face a daunting future, as reported by Blanchflower (2019):

> In one part of Rhyl, a seaside town in Wales, two-thirds of working-age people are dependent on out-of-work benefits.

(p. 2)

Such problems can be traced back to disengagement in school, especially at secondary level. In a classic study, *Learning to Labour*, Paul Willis (1977) showed how working-class youths' resistance to school, 'having a laff', 'messing about' and 'bunking off', led them inexorably into low-skilled work. Some graduates told us how hard it was to resist peer pressure and take academic work seriously in what are often referred to as 'sink schools'. Ironically, during the coronavirus lockdown, politicians of all parties lamented the impact missing school would have, particularly on disadvantaged children. Schools were presented as Utopian spaces where young people devoured knowledge with their friends. This contrasts sharply with the accounts of school offered to Wenham by her young interviewees:

> *There was nothing more I hated more than school...*
> *There was never a day without a fight...we always*
> *had supply teachers...All the teachers were always*
> *off;...you would walk in on a different teacher every*
> *single lesson.*

> *One young care-leaver, who stated bluntly 'school*
> *was crap', wrote a poignant rap poem:*

> *If I could go back and turn back time*

> *I would knuckle down and show it was my time to*
> *shine...*

> *In school I was always excluded*

> *People must think I'm hard and deluded.*

> *Going through school felt like I was on the wall of*
> *shame*

> *Because all I was going through was hurt and pain.*
>   (Wenham, 2020, pp. 51–52)

This exclusion from secure work of working-class youths, especially young men, has been a subject of concern since increased unemployment in the 1980s. Governments have tried to tackle the problem with a series of initiatives and programmes, among them the Youth Training Scheme (YTS), Bridging the Gap, Connexions, Modern Apprenticeships, Education Maintenance Awards (EMAs), but none of these have made much difference and all have now been scrapped. Indeed, in order to meet targets, those running the schemes often chose to recruit the less intractable cases. Such approaches relied on some kind of training or educational programme to help youths achieve employment. The short-comings of this strategy are pithily summarized by Simon Charlesworth in his striking study of Rotherham, a post-industrial former steel town blighted by unemployment: 'without economic change, an economic problem will not be solved by educational action' (Charlesworth, 2000, p. 152). There's no use being highly trained if there are no jobs to fill!

This situation has often been conceptualized controver-sially in terms of an *underclass*, a set of people permanently excluded and disengaged from formal economic activity. Such people were said to develop a culture of benefit dependence, were labelled as work-shy, and to pass these values on through generations (Murray, 1990, 1994). MacDonald and colleagues sought to test this on families with three genera-tions of unemployed members in two deprived areas, one in Glasgow and one in Middlesbrough. They found no trace of any families of this kind, but they did uncover profound deprivation. Rather than a 'culture of worklessness', people were stuck in a locality lacking in opportunities. The researchers identified a type of 'common social environment', which trapped youths and 'entrenched' them in disadvantage (MacDonald et al., 2020). Features of this environment included: ineffective training and education systems; declining local economy lacking secure jobs; neighbourhood decay and poor housing; poor health; a destructive local economy of crime and drugs and failed rehabilitation systems (2020, p. 19). Those of us who live in cities and large towns are likely to be able to name areas of this kind. The impact on the lives of youths is poignantly summed up in this statement from a young man aged 18 interviewed by Charlesworth, who transcribed his interviews in the dialect and accent of Rotherham:

> *A'm from a council estate...an' done time... in young offenders' places an' community service an' all kids doin' that shit ahr from council estates, an' wi'v got nowt guin' for us aht the'er, yer know what I mean? We've got no money, we've got no jobs, thi's just nothin' for us to do, we've got nowt. We'eras you look at kids up (middle-class location) wi' money, or whose parents 'ave got money; they've got a life an't thi? Ye see 'em rahnd tahn 'avin a good time wi' the'r trendy clothes and wot not, thi'v no need to gu aht thievin'.*

(Charlesworth, 2000, p. 171)

Such structures of disadvantage are likely to increase as youths and young adults feel the brunt of economic change, exacerbated by the pandemic. The Prince's Trust, Prince Charles' charity for young people, reported in January 2021 on its impact (Prince's Trust Mosaic (mosaicnetwork.co.uk)). The survey found that 25% of respondents were suffering mental ill health; 56% reported feeling anxious most of the time, rising to 64% among those not in education, employment or training. Almost half of these NEET young people said that they could see no end to their unemployment. This survey, the Trust's Tesco Youth Index carried out by the polling organization YouGov, recorded the bleakest findings of its twelve-year history:

*They face a disrupted education, a shrinking jobs
market and isolation from their loved ones, and as a
result, too many are losing all hope for the future. As
ever, it is unemployed young people, and those with
few qualifications and little confidence, who have an
even more negative experience.*

(Jonathan Townsend, Chief Executive, Prince's
Trust, 20 January 2021)

THE TRULY DISADVANTAGED? BLACK YOUTHS IN BRITAIN

Young people from Black and Minority Ethnic minority
(BAME) backgrounds have faced particular problems because
of the deeply seated racism in our society. This may take the
form of what is currently known as 'unconscious bias', attitudes and stereotypes of which we are hardly aware. The
position of BAME youths is a very good example of the use-
fulness of an intersectional perspective, as youth, ethnicity,
gender and class combine to produce very specific forms of
disadvantage.

Like their majority counterparts, young BAME Britons
have suffered from unemployment and lack of job opportunities, especially in economic downturns. Black Caribbean,
Pakistani and Bangladeshi youths have particularly high
unemployment rates. Government statistics for 2019 show
that unemployment is highest among the 16–24 age group,
but whereas for white youth the rate was 10%, for BAME
youths it was a worrying 19%.

As the second or third generation in migrant families,
youth in some BAME communities have often been seen as
being 'between two cultures', torn between community values
(such as religious observance and expectations of following

the family trade) and the more permissive values of white youth cultures. It is difficult to fit in comfortably with peer groups. For example, young Kurds and Turks in London told of being bullied at school by gangs of other ethnic groups, but at the same time resented being steered by their families into ethnic niche work: kebab houses for the boys and the garment industry for girls (Enneli et al., 2002). For such youths, HE may be an alternative route.

Such issues intersect with class and gender. American writers described the formation of a 'black bourgeoisie', (Frazier, 1965; Graham, 2000), African-Americans working in professions, as lawyers, educators, politicians and entrepreneurs. While there is less talk in the United Kingdom about the emergence of a BAME middle-class, it undoubtedly exists, particularly in public services, the voluntary sector and national and local government. In 2022 there are several Asian heritage cabinet ministers. Hospital footage during the pandemic showed that doctors of diverse ethnicities – Chinese, Indian and African – have become numerous in the NHS. There is strong pressure on children of such families to enter HE. Indian and Chinese parents in particular are often ambitious for their children to pursue careers in the traditional professions: medicine, pharmacy, law and accountancy. Bristol's elite schools contain significant numbers of Asian and Chinese pupils, but few African-Caribbeans. Shane, of mixed Anglo/Asian heritage who is discussed in Chapter 5, seems to be headed to the middle-class.

By contrast, working-class BAME youth may struggle to find work. The Joseph Rowntree Foundation in a recent report on poverty stated that 41% of Pakistani and Bangladeshi employees are found in low-skilled occupations; these groups have the highest unemployment rates. In addition, people from BAME groups are in and out of low-paid work more frequently than white counterparts (Weekes-Barnard, 2018).

African-Caribbean and Somali youths are also among the most disadvantaged. A teacher from a Bristol state school remarked to the *Winners and Losers* team:

> *There are certainly some African-Caribbean boys*
> *here whose fathers are into this and into that and into*
> *the other, and that's the way their lives and careers*
> *work. And that's how the boys see life going.*

This pattern of living is illustrated in a study carried out in a deprived working-class area of East London by Gunter and Watt (2009). They interviewed a number of young people, mostly African-Caribbean boys, and emphasized how important their particular locality or 'street' was to these young men as a source of information, activities and opportunities. They distinguished two particular cultures for earning a living, or at least 'getting by.' 'Grafting' was the term used for finding jobs in heavy manual work, such as cleaning, construction or docks. Such jobs were usually short-term, hard, but quite well-rewarded. They were often gained through personal contacts, family or friends, so this can be seen as a form of 'bonding' social capital. These jobs were for young men only, and the authors commented that these types of opportunity networks tended to be gender-homogeneous (p. 523). The other way of earning a living Gunter and Watt (2009) called 'road culture', activities, errands and 'missions' picked up on the street, This may include working in clubs and bars, with access to the music business as roadies, DJs or rappers, as is the case in some of Bristol's BAME communities.

A final transition route for youths was to attend college. Typically these young people aimed to escape by gain qualifications and access office or IT work, jobs in the care sector or as youth and play assistants. This presents early school-leavers with a second chance, for, like Wenham's interviewees, many regretted wasting their school years:

> *I hated school, but if I could go back I would behave*
> *so much. I'd sit down and do my work. I used to be*
> *naughty all the time.*
>   (Kandy, quoted Gunter & Watt, 2009, p. 521)

Young women were less likely than the males to drop out; gender is an issue, with different patterns in different ethnic communities. Young Indian women may carry their parents' professional aspirations into HE. Young Muslim women are also increasingly seen to be pursuing university education, especially at their local post-1992 institutions. Although older Pakistani and Bangladeshi women have very low participation rates, research in Oldham found that for economic reasons parents were encouraging daughters as well as sons to go to university (Dale & Shaheen, 1999). There were, however, constraints on the daughters' movements, as parents pressured them to 'live at home and commute to a local higher education institution' (p. 9). Sadly research shows that their progress into professional jobs may be hampered by the wearing of Islamic dress, as Islamophobia holds strong among recruiters (Bradley et al., 2007).

Such restrictions do not affect young women of African origin, although they too may well face racism blocking their progress. However, a number are building successful careers in public services and, especially, the voluntary sector. Others set up their own businesses. These ambitious young women form a significant part of the evolving 'black bourgeoisie'. In Angela McRobbie's term, they are part of a global cohort of 'top girls', resisting confinement to the precarious labour market (McRobbie, 2008; Ingram et al., forthcoming).

Despite some promising development, the continuance of racial discrimination in the labour market and the patterns of racial segregation will likely be heightened by the economic disruptions of the pandemic. BAME youth from working-class backgrounds may struggle in the aftermath to find secure employment. Sadly, but significantly, our sample of graduates contained few BAME young adults; the stories of two, Adele and Sariah, are told in Chapter 6 and are indicative of discrimination, significantly more than Shane who features in Chapter 5.

CONCLUSIONS

I think a lot of my generation feel how are they ever going to afford their own houses and have enough money...or have a stable enough job to have what (their parents) have... One of my friends is an illustrator and she just says, like so many of her friends are working in pubs and they've got degrees but there's nothing, there's no real way for them into the market to get a job.

This is how Hannah, whose story features in Chapter 4, reflected on the situation of Generation Y. This chapter has shown how these young women and men face a labour market bifurcated into, on the one hand, a minority of sought-after professional and business jobs, and on the other a precarious economy of low-paid, often temporary jobs: the 'low pay, no pay' economy.

While all young people may struggle for stability in such an economic climate, those from working-class youths typically fare the worst. Even those who succeed academically and access HE confront difficulties fitting into the university environment and are at a disadvantage in terms of their lack of economic and social capitals when they seek to build careers, as we shall see in Chapters 5 and 6.

In a world where success is often viewed in terms of individual talent and hard work, this book aims to demonstrate that this meritocratic claim is misplaced. What happens to individuals is strongly affected by their class, ethnicity and gender, as the stories in later chapters will illustrate. However, in the next chapter we briefly set the scene by describing the *Paired Peers* research, from which those stories are drawn, and place it in context within the city of Bristol and its two universities.

2

THE *PAIRED PEERS* PROJECT AND ITS FINDINGS

This chapter introduces the research discussed in this book. The stories told in the next four chapters are drawn from the *Paired Peers* project, which was funded by the Leverhulme Trust. The project was in two phases: the first phase, conducted by a team of academics from the University of Bristol (UoB) and the University of the West of England (UWE), followed an initial cohort of 90 students from the two universities through three years of undergraduate study to investigate how class impacted on the decisions they made and their student experience. After a one-year gap, we obtained funding for a further three years to study how these new graduates fared in building careers, drawing on the educational capital gained from their degrees. In this second phase, we followed 56 of the original cohort as they navigated their way through the precarious labour market; we could also explore the other aspects of the transition to adulthood, establishing stable emotional relationships and acquiring accommodation. Phase 1 commenced in 2010 and Phase 2 in

2014, so that the cohort entered university one year before fees rose from £3,290 to £9,000 a year, but experienced the impacts of the 2008 economic crash.

The overall aim of the study was to explore the impact of higher education (HE) on patterns of class division and social mobility. To do this we needed to compare various factors: the student's class background; the academic subject of their degree and the impact of attending an elite university (UoB) or a 'new' university (UWE, a former polytechnic). We needed to recruit matched pairs: for example, we selected eight students taking a Law degree: four from each university, made up of two students we identified as middle class and two as working class at each institution, so we could compare the classed pairs within and between universities.

This research design meant that we had to select students from subjects taught at both universities. We wanted a range of disciplines across Arts, Social Sciences and Natural Sciences, and some of which were more obviously career-oriented. We drew from 11 pairs of departments: Biology, Drama, Economics and Accounting, Engineering, English, History, Geography, Law, Politics, Psychology and Sociology. To recruit participants, we attended a lecture in the first week of term in each subject, explained the project and got students to fill in a short questionnaire collecting details to help us to identify their class background. We collected 2,130 questionnaires in total, but excluded mature students and overseas students, as they would bring in too many complexities around class definitions to be comparable. From the remaining questionnaires we selected our sample of 90 students.

As discussed earlier, class is a tricky and disputed concept. In line with our view that class is a nexus of social relationships, we chose a multidimensional approach to identifying working- and middle-class students: the type of schools they attended, their postcodes, their mothers' and fathers' occupations, whether they were the first generation in their family to attend university, whether most of their friends attended university, whether they received a bursary and their own self-definition of their class. Using these indicators, we grouped all students who had agreed to take part into three clusters: firmly middle-class, firmly working-class and what we termed 'the muddle in the middle', those not easy to categorize. Our cohort was chosen from the first two groups to offer the greatest level of contrast. The diagram below shows the class composition of the students who filled in our questionnaire. This reflects the different class composition of the student bodies of the two universities (Fig. 1).

There have been many studies of class and HE. What is unique in our research has been the pair design explained earlier and the intensive longitudinal nature of the project. The funding enabled us to employ research assistants to carry out numerous interviews. In Phase 1 the participants were inter-viewed twice each year: they completed diaries and timetables, took photos of their accommodation and marked-up maps showing their use of the city. Focus groups discussed gender issues. At the end of each year we held a party, enabling us to chat informally with those who attended. Some were invited to attend seminars and answer questions from the audience about their experiences. Inevitably we experienced drop-out, especially at the end of the first year, from students who either left the university or found taking part in the project too onerous. But most of those who stayed into the second year carried on until the third year: a total of 70 students. Many of these had established a strong rapport with their interviewers.

For Phase 2 we contacted all those remaining at the end of Phase 1: 56 agreed to take part. They were interviewed four times over the three years. Obviously, it was more difficult to interview them as they were now not concentrated in Bristol, but scattered around the country, and indeed a few were

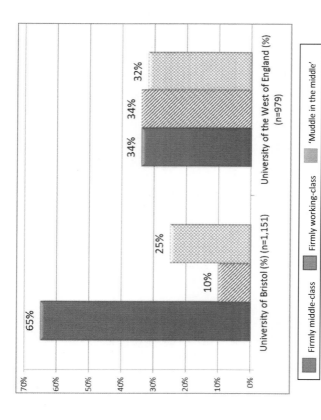

Fig. 1. The Class Composition of the Universities of Bristol and the West of England From Our Questionnaire Data.

abroad. Thus, a number had to be interviewed on Skype (sadly Zoom had not been invented!) or by telephone. We also asked them to create a mind map looking back on their student experience and, as part of the final interview, to construct a timeline showing the highs and lows of their life experiences. We met up with some of them at a final party in London after our final report's launch in 2017, to celebrate all they had done for us over the seven years.

THE CITY OF BRISTOL AND ITS TWO UNIVERSITIES

Bristol was the base for our study because the researchers worked at its two universities and were members of a Research Group exploring widening participation in HE. By Phase 2, the team had scattered around the country, just like the participants, an indication of the levels of geographical mobility typifying modern British economic life; only two of the original six-person project team members remained at their original university. Bristol was a good place for our project partly because of its two contrasting universities but also because it has long been a popular place to study. UoB is an elite Russell Group institution, seen in the second tier behind the 'Golden Triangle' of Cambridge, Oxford and London, while UWE is a mid-ranking institution drawing a high contingent of local students from its hinterland and is particularly attractive to those from local BAME communities.

Bristol city is a draw in its own right. It is known to have a lively music and cultural scene, with two theatres and a concert hall which attract prominent performers. It holds the world-famous Balloon Festival, along with a Harbour Festival and other local celebratory events. It is something of a gateway to the Glastonbury Festival. It houses two football teams, a highly rated rugby squad, a cricket ground visited by teams for one-day international matches and it is surrounded by attractive countryside within easy reach. It is also a student-friendly city, with a vibrant night-time economy featuring numerous bars, cafes and restaurants, which provide both entertainment and employment for students. Its night-clubs target student customers. In the centre of the city, the harbourside area is nightly packed with young revellers drinking. It is also known for its political radicalism, with frequent demonstrations, including recent climate change actions led by school and university students, and the 'kill the bill' demonstrations against restrictions on the public right to protest. While this book was being written, Bristol received worldwide attention when demonstrators pulled the statue of slave-owner Edward Colston from its plinth and threw it in the harbour.

But Bristol also has a darker side. It is a divided and segregated city, with affluent areas such as Clifton, Cotham, Redland and Stoke Bishop, where UoB is located and most of its students reside. Many of the wealthy inhabitants of these areas, including the students, will never set foot in some of the deprived areas of the city, such as Hartcliffe, Knowle West and Southmead, where poorer families live in large council estates. This was demonstrated when we asked our partici-pants to tell us about the parts of city they visited and indicate them on a map. Deprivation is also high in the inner-city areas where Bristol's BAME communities are clustered, St Paul's, Ashley and Easton, where rioting broke out in 1980. Between these areas and the grand houses of Clifton and Redland lies the Gloucester Road and Stokes Croft area, a lively, colourful highway, with a Banksy mural ('The Mild, Mild West', showing a teddy bear throwing a petrol bomb) and ranks of independent shops. This is the place of residence for many

UWE students who do not live in the university's own student village.

This divided nature of Bristol's geography and its contrasting urban spaces is mirrored in its two universities. UoB is a Russell Group university which has long been considered one of the United Kingdom's most prestigious. In 2010, 40% of UoB's student population had been previously educated outside of the state education system, a proportion almost six times greater than the national average of 7% (Department for Education, 2010). Zoe, a Law student, told us that she was the only person on the corridor in her hall of residence who had attended a state school. The university's many sites and buildings are mainly located in the affluent parts of the city; the Wills Memorial Building, which houses the Law Department alongside the Great Hall where degree ceremonies are held, is a city landmark, a Victorian Gothic tower.

By contrast, UWE is mainly sited on a large purpose-built campus on the edge of the city, where it shades into South Gloucestershire. The campus contains its own student village, where most first years are accommodated. It attracts many local students, including considerable numbers of British Black and Asian young people. The class composition of the two universities is very different. According to the Sutton Trust, in 2010 when our participants started university, 34% of UWE students came from manual or routine family backgrounds, as opposed to only 14% of UoB students. Further, in 2010 UWE admitted twice as many part-time students and nine times more mature students as UoB, as reported by the HE Statistics Agency (2012).

There is a degree of rivalry between the two student bodies, reflected in intervarsity matches. Ned, a Law student from UWE, told us, 'we call them Ras, and they think of us as thick'. As the stories in succeeding chapters show, some upper-middle-class students may feel out of place at UWE, especially those who were privately educated. Oscar, a Politics student, told us that when asked where he went to university he simply stated 'Bristol' to cover up the stigma he felt at attending an 'ex-poly'. Such stigma lasts; UWE ceased being 'a poly' and became a university in 1992, the same year most of our participants were born!

CLASSED AND GENDERED TRANSITIONS: KEY PROJECT FINDINGS

The findings of the project are summarized in two reports that can be found on the *Paired Peers* website (Phase one report: https://www.bristol.ac.uk/media-library/sites/spais/migrated/documents/report.pdf Phase two report: https://pairedpeers2.uwe.ac.uk/pdfs/Key%20findings_executive%20summary.pdf). The research team co-authored a book from phase one of the project (Bathmaker et al., 2016), and a second book from phase two is about to be published (Ingram et al., forthcoming). Here we summarize a few of the key points from both phases which are relevant to the stories told in the next four chapters.

Phase 1

We analyzed the findings of the first phase in three stages: 'getting in', 'getting on' and 'getting out'. In each case we observed class differences.

In terms of 'getting in' there was clear middle-class advantage, while working-class youths face barriers. As we saw in Chapter 1, going to university has become a taken-for-granted part of middle-class life. Young people are assisted by parents and teachers, who pass on their knowledge about universities and courses to their children and assist with the application process. Private schools or highly academic state schools coach students to apply to specific universities; some teachers may have direct links to Oxbridge colleges and elite universities such as UoB.

By contrast, some of our working-class undergraduates spoke of attending schools like those discussed in Chapter 1. Some noted that other pupils were ill-disciplined and uninterested in learning. In such schools, guidance towards HE is less embedded, so, for example, students may fail to make the right choices of GCSEs and A levels to pursue specific degree choices, as Anna, a working-class History student, indicated:

> *No-one even told me that if I wanted to do medicine I had to take the sciences and maths. They didn't prepare me at all.*

On the other hand, pupils who stand out from the mass of their peers in their interest in specific subjects may catch the attention of teachers and receive encouragement. They may, however, be steered towards less prestigious universities. Parents who have not been to university themselves cannot give much help in choice of institution. Because of this lack of 'insider knowledge', plus the emotional and economic costs of travelling away, working-class young people are more likely to end up in a university close to home.

In terms of 'getting on' in an academic sense, the class gap seemed to diminish. Many of our participants spoke of the difficulty of adjusting to the more independent style of learning at university, contrasting it with the 'spoon-feeding' they had received at school. In fact, working-class students may be at an advantage, as they have had to work hard and overcome difficulties to reach university that many of their middle-class peers did not encounter. For instance, Marcus, a working-class student at UoB, commented:

*There is definitely a way of life associated with
people who have been to boarding school, private
school… However, I actually feel they've gained no
advantage – or very little advantage – from the
experience and the price of their education. I
constantly get reassured in the fact that I have similar
grades to them, but when it comes to dealing with life
shall we say, I seem to get on better than them and
it's them coming to me for advice.*

Those from less privileged backgrounds tended to be more
sensible in organizing their lifestyles, and particularly in
handling their finances, given experiences of tight budgets.
Samantha, also at UoB, was critical of her public-school peers:

*They just spend money like it grows on trees … go
out and go shopping and buy more clothes and I'm
like 'but you have a wardrobe full of clothes, you
don't need any more'.*

At the end of the three years, the working-class students in
our sample achieved as good degree results as the
middle-class, with a significant number gaining first-class
degrees. There is a caveat here though: we suspect our sample represented the keener, more serious sort of students who
elected to join our study. Those who dropped out of our study
may have been less academically successful. We know that
historically working-class students are more likely to drop
out: several of our recruits did leave, deciding that university
was 'not for the likes of them', they had made a bad choice or
that they missed home too much (see Bradley, 2017).

Despite their academic achievements, most of our
working-class participants were only able to gain limited other
forms of capital from their undergraduate years to enhance
their CVs. This was because of practical obstacles: most of

them had to work in the summer vacations, so could not take up placements and internships or volunteering opportunities in developing countries as, for example, could Hannah, whose story is told in Chapter 4. Moreover, the extra-curricular activities (ECAs) which adorn a CV are expensive for those on restricted budgets; while restrictions on free time were imposed by the need to take paid work during term time. Thus they could not play by the 'rules of the game' (Bathmaker et al., 2013), rules perfectly articulated in the following comment from Joanna, a middle-class student at UWE:

> *The reason I volunteer at St John's Ambulance now is because it will look good on my CV. And obviously I enjoy it, but the reason I started it was because it looks good on my CV and the guy I work with is brilliant for giving me references and things like that…. But yeah, that's what I've spent my 3 years doing, is making sure I've got a CV worth having when I leave, because obviously there's a lot more competition for graduate jobs than there used to be and graduate is a sort of baseline that you then look at your CV to build upon.*

These issues were reflected in what happened to the students in terms of their destinations on 'getting out' of university. In the third year, 70 students remained in the study, seven of whom were staying on to complete a final year in a four-year degree course; we completed 'exit' interviews with 59. The table below shows what their position was at the time of that interview, mostly conducted in the Spring Term of the final year. Figures are given in percentages to make a balanced comparison because of the different numbers in each category (Table 1).

As the table shows, working-class students were lagging behind, less likely to have a destination fixed. The only

Table 1. Destinations of Students, by University, Class and Gender in Percentages.

Percentage in each category	UoB (n = 34)	UWE (n = 25)	Middle-Class (n = 33)	Working-Class (n = 26)	Women (n = 35)	Men (n = 24)	Total (n = 59)
Secured graduate job	15	0	9	8	3	17	9
Secured PGCE place	15	8	9	12	17	0	10
Secured other study place	12	4	12	4	9	8	9
Secured summer placement	9	12	15	4	6	17	10
No destination yet secured	52	76	55	72	65	58	62

exception was in the proportion proceeding to a Postgraduate Certificate in Education (PGCE) a teacher training qualification. As mentioned earlier, teaching became a favoured destination for some working-class young women. We also noticed a drift towards teaching among middle-class women students, who might be deterred by the competitiveness surrounding elite graduate jobs. The table also indicates that those attending UoB were more likely to have secured a future destination, as discussed in the next section.

Phase 2

In some respects, the lives of our participants converged when they were students, despite the differences sketched out above. As undergraduate students they shared a status and their core activities were of a similar nature whatever their class of origin. However, as graduates their paths soon began to diverge quite dramatically. These divergences sprang from the three aspects of our pairing strategy: their class background and the capitals derived from it; whether they attended an elite 'old' university or a post-1992 and the academic discipline studied.

Certain degrees give access more directly to employment. The most vocational subject we studied was Engineering. All our graduates but one found jobs in engineering, the young men found work more quickly than the women and were promoted much faster (Papafilippou & Bentley, 2017). This is a degree that offers notable employability if wanted, and was one area where class appeared to make no difference. We could label it the most meritocratic destination.

At the other end of the spectrum, graduates with arts degrees often struggled to settle into careers. While Drama students aspired to work as actors or be involved in the production side of theatre, these are highly competitive areas and ones marked by insecurity (as the pandemic drastically confirmed). Only one member of our Drama cohort ended up working in a theatrical context. A second worked for a time as box-office manager for a theatre, but ended up in a quite different occupation, an artisan food company; both were middle-class. Where no obvious occupational choice appears, the graduates tend to drift for a time, often with long-term aspirations for writing, journalism, taking a PhD and so forth. Sometimes the drift leads to teaching, particularly for our female participants.

Secondly, the university attended has a strong impact on outcomes. As the table showed, 15% of our UoB sample were fixed up with a graduate job by their final undergraduate interview, as opposed to none from UWE, and 24% had secured places for further study or for a PGCE, twice the 12% from UWE. This may partly reflect the competitive atmosphere at UoB but also results from the University of Bristol 'cachet'; recruiters see a UoB degree as a sign of calibre. UoB graduates are more likely to end up with major companies than UWE students and more likely to move to London for work as explained below. This is acknowledged by the UWE careers staff, who often target their students at smaller, local organizations.

However, it is difficult to disentangle the university effect from class advantage and disadvantage. There are two important factors which help graduates to obtain top jobs: internships and placements, often unpaid, and personal contacts. An internship at a top finance company or law firm can be a route into a permanent job, and if not it is nonetheless valuable as CV material. Working-class graduates, however, cannot afford to take unpaid internships, as their parents lack economic capital. Also many had to take paid work in the vacations. Further, working-class students lacked social capital that could be used to find graduate-level work. As the stories will show, many middle-class graduates had relatives or acquaintances who could smooth the pathway into a desired job.

Another crucial class issue is the London factor. The capital acts as a magnet for ambitious graduates, as top jobs are concentrated there (Canary Wharf, the City law and finance firms, the Civil Service, media and the arts, headquarters of voluntary organizations). However, rents in London are so exorbitant that unless their family home is there or the family can help with costs, graduates cannot afford to live there. Instead many working-class young adults had to return to the places where they grew up, such as Zoe, who studied Law at UoB, but ended back living with parents in Wales where opportunities were fewer. Another example was Jasmine, a UWE Sociology student who returned to Cornwall, where graduate job openings are negligible. Jasmine spent some time unemployed before finding work as a care assistant; she worried about ever acquiring a graduate job (see Ingram et al., forthcoming, for details of Zoe's and Jasmine's stories).

In general, middle-class graduates are cushioned from the cruel circumstances of the current labour market. Families can help with the expenses of internships, training or further study and provide comfortable living circumstances in pleasant neighbourhoods if young graduates are forced to return home. Indeed, some of our middle-class participants, especially young women, chose to spend time 'back home' exploring employment opportunities before settling on a career path. Waller (2011) referred to this as 'the glass floor', an invisible barrier preventing downward social mobility for the socially and economically advantaged. By contrast, the working-class graduates felt the pressure to find work immediately, some in secure jobs such as primary school teaching, others taking less skilled work in order to start earning. While middle-class graduates can delay their choices (for example, Mark, who chose to go motorcycling around the Far East doing temporary teaching work), the working-class young people are compelled to be more pragmatic, if they want to avoid having to access welfare support.

The stories of the graduates we tell in Chapters 3–6 highlight the processes outlined in this section. We have chosen to concentrate on a few of our participants as a way of bringing to life the struggles faced by Generation Y; their stories, we believe, will illuminate the plight faced by so many. As Ken Plummer puts it 'stories help us to imagine, animate and value human life' (2019, p. viii), whilst Andrew Sparkes suggested such biographical accounts 'illuminate the social context of individual lives' (2003, p. 3).

TELLING PEOPLE'S STORIES

Story-telling, or *narrative,* is intrinsic to human life. Every civilization has its storytellers, be it a shaman, a court poet, a television script writer or a digital blogger. Stories are told through pictures, poems and songs, plays, books and novels, films, even still photographs. 'Every picture tells a story', we say. The famous photograph of Phan Thị Kim Phúc, a small child running down a road with her clothes on fire told a poignant story of the suffering napalm inflicted on civilians during the Vietnam war. As we write this, pictures from Afghanistan show terrified boys clinging to the outside of aeroplanes and mothers throwing babies into the airport over rolls of barbed wire.

Stories are an important way that people learn about the world they inhabit and relate to the experiences of others. They are a repository of knowledge, so it is not surprising that narrative method has become a popular tool within sociology, especially the collecting of life stories. Qualitative research commonly involves the capture and analysis of participants' stories of aspects of their experiences of the phenomena under study. As Barbara Czarniawska states, 'a student of social life...needs to become interested in narrative as a form of social life, a form of knowledge and a form of communication'. (2004, p. 13). The currently fashionable practice of *autoethnography* involves social researchers constructing narrative accounts of their own life or elements of their experiences.

In the project, our first interview with the undergraduates was an unstructured one, we asked them to tell the story of how they came to be a student at UoB or UWE. As far as possible, we wanted them to narrate in their own words how and why they ended up in their particular course of study. We tried to intervene as little as we could, but where people were shy or found it difficult to reflect back on their lives, we would prompt them with appropriate questions: 'how did you get on at school?'; 'did your mum and dad help you?', 'tell us a bit more about that'. As the project progressed and the participants got to know their interviewers and feel comfortable with them, they would tell us unprompted stories about things that happened to them.

Of course, when people look back on their lives, they are *reconstructing* events and putting their own interpretation on them. They may misremember some aspects of the past. Sometimes they will tell an interviewer what they think s/he wants to hear! Narratives, then, do not just reflect, but also create past experiences. Nonetheless, reading these interviews carried out over a time period of seven years, we noted how consistent the accounts offered by our interviewees often appeared to be.

Analysis of life narratives often involves the identification of what sociologists call *critical moments*, experiences that result in significant changes in direction. For example, in the *Winners and Losers* project, Pearl, an African-Caribbean woman, who worked as a hotel cleaner, told us how a manager recognized her abilities and set her on a pathway into management; another respondent told us how joining the Sea Scouts had diverted him from adolescent misbehaviour. Often a family member or friend may play a pivotal role. Thus, analysis of narratives can offer important insights about change. Ken Plummer's *Telling Sexual Stories* (1994) charts the prevalence of stories in the mass media, showing how narrative is involved both in how individuals construct their own sexual identities and how societies' attitudes to sexuality change; so that, for example, transsexuality has become in Britain a legitimate and protected form of identity (Plummer, 2019). Plummer tells how the 'counter-narrative' of 'Gay Pride' challenging the traditional stigmatization of homosexuality allowed him to 'come out' as a young gay man.

The stories we present in the following chapters are constructs: they emerge from dialogues between the researcher and research participant; the participant provides raw data, but the researcher steers and then analyzes it, relating it to identified themes. To write these chapters we re-read all the interviews with each graduate whose story was selected. With such a wealth of material it is impossible to do justice to every rich nuance, but we believe that, because of our immersion in this material, the narratives we have constructed present a fair picture of the experiences of these young adults. The interpretations, of course, are ours.

We end this chapter with three short narratives of our own, explaining the pathways which led us to the *Paired Peers* project. These constitute a kind of autoethnographic experiment, placing ourselves in the frame of the research and acknowledging our own positionality and values towards the issues covered.

TELLING OUR STORIES

Harriet: *The Crown of My Academic Career*

My life has been one of ups and downs, disappointments, lucky breaks, achievements, setbacks; but I ended up a professor of sociology and leading the *Paired Peers* project.

I grew up in Cambridge in an impoverished middle-class family, but one rich in cultural capital. At school I was a rebel, always in trouble, but excelling in exams. My younger Brother and Sister both went to Oxford University but I chose to go to Bristol, although I failed to win a place on the Drama course (I dreamed of being an actress) and ended up studying English. Three fabulous years were filled with parties, friendships, romances, political activism, acting, singing in choirs and operas. I didn't get a good enough degree to go on to a PhD as I had hoped, so ended up doing a PGCE. I moved to Leicester where I worked in a sports shop, the Gas Board and a clock factory, before finally finding a job in a secondary school where I stayed for some years. Later there was a messy bit of my life, when I got ill with post-viral syndrome, had to give up teaching and tried to write novels. My marriage broke up, but by then I had embarked on another degree as a sociologist. This was the start of a new life.

My new career as a sociologist took me to jobs in Durham (where I met a new partner), Sunderland and finally back to Bristol University as a teacher. By then I had started to publish in my fields of research: work, gender and class. At Bristol I secured funding for several projects, including *Winners and Losers,* which looked at young adults' careers and *Double Disadvantage,* exploring the work experiences of ethnic minority women. My interests always lay in divisions of class, gender and ethnicity. All the projects involved teams because I love working with others; bouncing ideas off them is so exhilarating. My interest in class led me to the widening participation research network, bringing together academics and administrators from UoB and UWE. Out of this grew the idea of the *Paired Peers* project. I put in for a three-year grant with Leverhulme Trust, emphasizing my career-long interest in the dynamics of class, with Richard, Ann-Marie and Tony as co-researchers and was thrilled to succeed. We employed two researchers, Nicola and Jody and when Jody left to have a baby,

Jessie and Phoebe took over. What a team! The research was so enjoyable and the team worked so well together, we put in for another three years, and got it! By now I was employed part-time at UWE, being past retirement age. This was my last funded research project, and it has been a delight and joy to work with such a great team (Laura, Vanda and Mike joined us at UWE), studying the lives of such inspiring members of Generation Y.

Richard: *On the Home Straight*

I was born in the East London/Essex border area, the eldest of two children of a bright working-class couple who had both 'passed' their 11+ exam. My Dad left school and followed many of his male relatives into Fords motor company in Dagenham, the major local employer, albeit as a technical apprentice rather than working on the production line like his own father and uncles had. My Mum had a number of routine white-collar jobs before settling down as a housewife and mother when I was born within a few days of her 21st birthday. My Sister followed 18 months later, and by then we had moved from our rented flat in Barking to a council house in the 1960s Essex new town of Basildon after my Dad re-located to the tractor manufacturing division of Fords which was based there.

When I was four we moved to another Essex town, Benfleet, where I went to school and lived until I moved to Bristol to study Sociology and Politics at the Polytechnic (now UWE). When I took my degree in the mid-1980s fewer than 20% of young people did so, meaning my choice was fairly unusual for someone from my background. Most of my school friends didn't stay beyond 16, and by no means all of those who did actually progressed further to study at degree level. I was the first in my family to do so after making a conscious choice not to follow my Dad into Fords, nor my Uncle into the London's docks, as I could through a traditional 'inherited' right for these well-paid, unionized blue-collared jobs. Nor did I fancy the life of commuting into London daily on the train to work in the finance sector either as many of my more academically capable peers had chosen to; I wanted something more intellectually stimulating.

I was aware at a relatively young age how empowering education could be and how it could offer choices that were otherwise denied to most of us, including my wider family and most of my school friends. I was a reasonably good but by no means brilliant student, and I got my 2:1 degree. After a year working as an elected student union sabbatical officer I joined the civil service through their graduate scheme since I wanted to work in a socially useful public sector job. I liked the idea of teaching adults one day, but felt I should experience something of life outside the education system first. After six years in the civil service I left and went to Cardiff University to train as a further education (FE) lecturer, and I worked for several years in a number of part-time FE teaching roles in and around Bristol. I then decided to move into HE teaching and took a Sociology Master's degree part-time, before winning a PhD bursary for a study of the impact of returning to education on a cohort of mature students.

I got a full-time lecturing job at UWE in 2003, and was by now married and a father to two small boys. My interest in both promoting social justice and the impact of education on peoples' lives continued, and led to me getting involved in the cross-university widening participation research group where I met Harriet and Tony from UoB, and along with my UWE colleague Ann-Marie we developed the plans for the *Paired Peers* project. Now, as a professor approaching the latter stages of my working life, and nearly a dozen years since the start of *Paired Peers*, I feel confident that it's likely to remain in the research of which I'm most proud, as well as being a fantastic way to meet and work with so many like-minded people. Not just the other researchers, or the participants whose lives it has been a genuine privilege to follow, but the numerous people with whom I've been able to share this fascinating project, including fellow researchers at conferences, policy makers we've advised and my own students with whom I've discussed it.

Laura: *Still climbing*

I grew up in Barnsley, South Yorkshire, in a working-class family. Though I flitted between households, I spent most of my adolescence living with two of my Brothers and my Dad, who was an engineer before he was made redundant. My Mum did various jobs which she could do around raising my third Brother. Over the years she has worked as a cleaner, a fast food server and school cook, and as a dinner lady.

I spent my youth engaged in rich working-class cultural practices: playing pool and darts in the pub, hanging out with my mates around Barnsley market and holidaying in caravans in Bridlington. Though I never went to bed hungry, financial anxiety radiated through both of my parent's households. Due to these factors, university was not an expected transition for me. My Dad initially refused to sign the forms that would allow me to get a student loan, and he said 'it's too expensive! Plus, who's going to look after your brothers? Why don't you get an apprenticeship as a typist or something like your Mum did?'.

After much difficult negotiation I got the signature. While this might be an ordinary moment to those from more affluent backgrounds, this was a life-defining moment that I'll never forget. To get the signature I had to agree that I would stay at home while I studied and that I would go to a university close by. My UCAS application was populated by post-92 universities in neighbouring cities, a common 'choice' made by other working-class students.

I chose to study a degree in English and Education Studies at Sheffield Hallam University with the aspiration to become a secondary English teacher who could make a positive impact on the lives of young working-class people in Barnsley. After submitting my final year dissertation it was recommended by my supervisor that I consider applying for PhD funding. At the time, I had never heard of a PhD, and after looking into it I sensed it wasn't a route for 'people like me'. Besides, I'd already been offered a job teaching in a Further Education setting in Barnsley. After some to-ing and fro-ing with my supervisor I thought, 'what's the harm in submitting an application?'

A few weeks later, I was begging my Nan for £200 to help me move to Bristol to start my PhD. Further study was on the horizon! I embarked on my PhD and my new role as a research assistant on the *Paired Peers* project with mixed emotions: Thrilled to have the opportunity to carry on researching social inequalities and excited about my future possibilities. However, I was concerned about those who felt that I had 'left them behind'. I felt like a class traitor, and still do to a certain degree, which is a common feeling experienced by working-class academics.

3

REACHING FOR THE TOP: MIDDLE-CLASS MEN'S WORK STORIES

We start the story of our graduate outcomes with the middle-class men, as our data show them to be the undoubted labour market 'winners' of the four groups we discuss. They were most likely to have a clear idea of their career objectives and to leave university having already accessed their graduate paths, through having a job or place on a graduate scheme, a placement or internship that would easily lead to a job, or being signed up for postgraduate study. Like the middle-class women in Chapter 4, they tended to possess social contacts which helped them find employment and to be aware of the expected cultural behaviours which facilitated them gaining graduate work. However, not all middle-class men conform to this 'winning' pattern. Some rebelled and refused to 'play the graduate game' (Bathmaker et al., 2013). Others, especially those who have studied humanities subjects, are uncertain of their career direction. We tell both types of stories in this chapter. We also take care to distinguish between fractions of the middle-class here, since the story is more nuanced than the simple binary demarcation between the working- and middle-classes, as this and the three following chapters demonstrate.

This chapter features the narrative accounts of four middle-class young men. Lloyd, who studied English and Drama at UWE, and Adrian, who studied Economics at UoB, were both lower-middle class. Although neither was first generation in their families to attend university (all the parents had) they were generally less 'established' than some other middle-class participants in terms of status, wealth and income. The other two young men in this chapter, Sebastian (Geography, UoB) and Dylan (Politics, UWE), had fairly wealthy families, and Sebastian attended a fee-paying boarding school. Dylan went to a high-performing state school in a wealthy area of the home counties; both had parents and other older family members who had been to university. Thus, they possessed the knowledge and necessary resources – more of the valuable economic, cultural and social capitals – to take full advantage of university study and could 'concertedly cultivate' their CVs, using their advantages to pursue career interests and ambitions. These upper-middle-class young men were consequently better placed to further benefit from their time at university than their lower-middle-class and, particularly, their working-class peers, as this chapter will explain.

LLOYD: 'I JUST WANT TO STAY BEING A CHILD AS LONG AS POSSIBLE, AND NOT BE AN ADULT AT ALL, EVER'

Lloyd grew up in a small town in the generally wealthy county of Surrey, although his family was not especially well-off; Lloyd's father worked as an IT network manager for a transport company, and his mother was an occupational therapist; both had attended university. Lloyd had one younger sister who was still at school when he started at on the Drama and English course at UWE in 2010, but who subsequently went to university. In his first year Lloyd lived in the cheapest hall of residence on campus, nicknamed 'Council Court' and considered below the standard of other halls. He never came across as an especially enthusiastic or committed student during the seven years of interviews with him. He talked at the initial meeting of deciding to attend university as a way of avoiding more 'adult' responsibilities, and this was a recurring theme in each interview up to 2017:

> *It's always been expected that I'd go to uni I think, and I've never dreamed of not going to uni because that's too scary, to start work and all that kind of stuff. So yeah, basically (I) just want to stay being a child as long as possible and not be an adult at all, ever.*

He talked of being 'bored at home', and enjoying living in a city with its enhanced access to his favourite cultural activities – theatre and live music, for instance. Going to university was a way to enjoy this. He spoke of lacking self-confidence to work full-time in the theatre business; he liked acting, but felt it was 'a bit clichéd'. In his second year, Lloyd talked of moving into teaching as an obvious decision for him after graduating, and the idea of working with underprivileged children particularly appealed, as he appreciated the blatant inequalities of the UK's education system. He had discovered the Teach First scheme, whereby undergraduates like him could go and work in a school with children from disadvantaged backgrounds. In theory, this appealed to him but during his first year at university he had been unsure of such a future; indeed, at times he was explicit that he did not want to teach, although he was somewhat conflicted:

> *But I don't really want to become a teacher, I don't*
> *want to follow the whole English straight to teacher*
> *route, which might happen, but it seems like the easy*
> *route and the logical route*

At a later interview with Lloyd, it was apparent that teaching remained of interest to him, but we sensed he was never committed enough to the idea of teaching to actually do it:

> *Realistically I'm kind of looking at teaching I guess.*
> *I've been told I've got quite a lot of patience so that*
> *would be a good thing...organizational skills would*
> *probably be useful, which I'm not sure I necessarily*
> *have the right ones but I think that's an option. And I*
> *like kids, I get along with them usually. So yeah I*
> *think that's a possibility.*

Whilst the notion of teaching remained an option, albeit not an especially attractive one, Lloyd was unsure which age group appealed to him the most:

> *I feel primary school is too young in a way...*
> *Secondary school, I think it's also where you lose*
> *more kids from the educational system. I mean in my*
> *school a lot of people dropped out in year 9....And*
> *then people lose interest and they're going to lose*
> *interest in secondary school rather than primary*
> *school. It's weird, because I remember being in*
> *secondary school and watching supply teachers and*
> *thinking "oh God I don't want to do that ever",*
> *because it just looked painful, especially if you had*
> *like a rough class. But at the same time I kind of feel*
> *those are classes which are more worthwhile in a*
> *way....I don't know what you call it, the careers day,*
> *like at (university campus), I talked to a bloke*

> *from...I think he described it as kind of like a charity*
> *called Teach First, where....they take students, they*
> *take just graduated students and take them to...poor*
> *areas where they don't have much attendance and*
> *stuff and try and get them to put their enthusiasm for*
> *their course across to the other students, to try and*
> *increase like, I suppose, people from poor areas*
> *getting into education, which I think's really*
> *important, I think it's really good.*

Despite liking the idea of teaching in principle, and certainly valuing it as an important role in society, Lloyd sometimes felt that he lacked the self-confidence for it:

> *I mean whether I could actually stand up in front of a*
> *class of people who don't want to be there and*
> *probably hate my guts, I don't know, I'm not 100%*
> *sure. But at the same time I think it's something that*
> *would be worthwhile doing, and it would be really*
> *good and I'd feel proud of doing that I think. But*
> *whether it would be good for my mental health or*
> *anything I don't know.*

Lloyd was a keen musician who played in bands throughout his time at university (and subsequently after graduating). He also liked writing and suggested journalism appealed to him as a possible career choice too. He specifically explored the notion of becoming a music journalist, and took a short course on it, which also involved attending a festival and writing a review of bands he saw there for a national newspaper work-experience training scheme. Lloyd also got an opportunity to work for a day with a local BBC TV culture show, and the chance to work in the summer on an internship with them.

Even towards the end of his time as an undergraduate, Lloyd remained ambivalent towards his career options:

> *I don't know…the idea of having one career for life just sounds very dead end, very like "this is what you're doing, stick with it because you don't have any other options". Having said that, I don't know why I feel like that because both my parents have, and it's not like I've had early influences of them changing jobs a lot, because I don't think they ever have been out of work at all…which is lucky obviously, very lucky. I just want to be one of those people who's done everything in a way - which is not going to happen…I think being a teacher for the rest of my life is a bit weird so….I've never really known what I'm going to do after uni, so the idea of being unemployed for a bit just seems realistic…Obviously I'd like to be able to have a career, move out of my home, have my own house, get a car ASAP, but I don't know if that's going to happen….realistically.*

Lloyd returned to his family home in Surrey after graduating and took a number of short-term and part-time jobs, but then came back to Bristol and moved in with some friends from university. He had secured a position on a graduate internship in a Communications and Marketing Department, a role which eventually turned into a permanent position. This role involved working with journalists, both briefing and being interviewed by them and speaking on behalf of the employer. He was still considering taking a postgraduate journalism course, and had now dismissed the notion of teaching.

When we last heard from Lloyd in autumn 2021 he was still living in Bristol, renting a property with his partner, and working as a media relations officer for a government body, a secure and permanent role and earning around £35,000.

Lloyd differed significantly from the other middle-class young men whose narratives feature in the chapter in a number of ways. He lacked the clear 'sense of entitlement', drive or self-confidence of the two upper-middle-class participants, Sebastian and Dylan, and also the career focus both Dylan and Adrian demonstrated throughout their period of involvement with the project. For Lloyd, university was a means of deferring adulthood and the increase in responsibilities that would inevitably accompany it, a largely middle-class approach to life; he didn't face the economic imperative to earn a living as many working-class young men in Chapter 5 did.

ADRIAN: A SOCIALLY CONSCIOUS ECONOMIST

Adrian, who grew up in inner-city London and attended what he characterized as a fairly rough and generally low-achieving comprehensive school, studied Economics at UoB. He estimates that from his school year group of around 300 students, only about 40 progressed to university; this contrasts with Lloyd's school where the majority progressed to university, and both Sebastian and Dylan's schools, where just about everyone did. Adrian's parents are Irish immigrants 'the children of cleaners and factory workers', with his mother working as a primary school teacher, and his father as a quantity surveyor. Like Lloyd at UWE, Adrian also lived in the cheapest student accommodation at UoB, and his residence was known disparagingly as 'Poverty Hall'. Each was comfortable with their decision to choose the accommodation they did, both at the time, and subsequently, when reflecting back on their time as a student.

Talking to us during his first year, Adrian suggested his
career goals were reasonably broad, but had a clear public
service or charity sector focus:

> *It changes a fair bit, but I'm looking a lot at the
> moment into trying to get work in charities and
> development, or maybe working in Government in
> like the Economic Service or the Diplomatic Service
> or something like that. But hopefully something that
> I might be able to travel a bit would be kind of the
> area that I would be looking to getting into. And I
> think International Development is what I'm kind of
> leaning towards, that sort of development
> organization in charities.*

Adrian worked in bars to help fund his way through university, since he felt he couldn't afford not to. This issue
framed his disposition towards internships too. He realized
how valuable they were in terms of securing the type of work
he was interested in, but, like many of our working-class
participants, did not feel he could afford to do them:

> *I think for a few weeks I really tried to look into
> internships but...I think there's been loads in the
> press about it recently as well, that you can't get an
> internship in a lot of fields unless you can afford to
> not earn any money, and I don't think I can....I can't
> afford to get an internship in the charities or some of
> the NGOs and stuff...they won't pay, so I mean I'm
> going to have to sort out getting a job... I'd prefer
> not to do any more bar work over the summer, it just
> kind of ruins your social life!*

Adrian suggested his parents were quite left-wing politi-
cally, and committed union members and he broadly shared
their political opinions. He was disappointed that many of his
fellow Economics students at UoB saw the course primarily as

a route into a well-paid job in finance, rather than doing something he considered socially valuable, and also that the university careers guidance service seemed to echo that:

> *Because as soon as you click "economics"...it narrows everything down to investment banking, consultancy, accountancy or law... And I can't imagine anything worse than any of those jobs. And I got dragged along yesterday, there was a Careers Fair at...Wills Memorial Building...and it was just terrible, everyone turning up dressed up in suits...I cannot imagine working in that sector. But that's the problem...as soon as you say that you do economics to any careers advice people, or online, then it immediately just kind of discounts everything (else).*

To Adrian's frustration, even the government careers' portal seemed to suggest that working in a commercial environment presupposed a lack of concern for the bigger social issues that he was interested in:

> *I had a funny thing actually, the government like jobs website prospects, I went on there and did like a 30 minute test, and there's a section where it talks about what you want out of your career. And you can either pick...you can either be...'altruistic' can be your major point that you want, or you can pick like being 'commercial'. ...From knowing economics, I like the idea of running a business or something like that, I wanted to be in commercial, but I also wanted to do something that had a good social impact. So I clicked altruistic as well and it immediately flashes up red, as like "you cannot do this in life".*

The appeal of both studying and working abroad was strong, and he had a real desire to experience life in different countries. Although he didn't do so, he considered spending a semester in his second undergraduate year in Madrid; however, he did undertake postgraduate study abroad, as outlined below. His girlfriend in Bristol was Norwegian, and he enjoyed travelling with her. Towards the end of his second year at university, Adrian's thoughts were turning to possible postgraduate study as a way of helping secure the type of work he was most interested in. Whilst he retained thoughts of working in a government or other official organization, he had considered other options based upon his personal interests:

> *Either...something...Civil Service related, or kind of department of development that sort of thing, but obviously that's quite hard to get into and you often need a PhD....I'd have to see after doing a Master's obviously if I wanted to do that. Other than that it would be...kind of thinking about doing things in the stuff that I'm just more interested for myself, within the music industry or something. I've been in touch with a few different companies, I don't know if you know Spotify? and those sort of things, seen internships there, and I'm looking into the Google internship scheme, but that's quite tricky because they only recruit Oxbridge undergrads.*

Adrian spoke of applying for a range of internships previously, without necessarily thinking through the longer term implications of working for the companies or in the industries concerned:

> *I had a John Lewis internship, it's like a retail management thing, and I applied because I like the*

> *company, John Lewis, their ethics, but I've just got
> no interest in retail management, and I kind of did
> it....I'd applied for a Rolls Royce one and I was
> considering some consultancy firms, and I was
> thinking when I did that 'what am I doing, I don't
> want to be a consultant or anything'. And it's just
> this whole rat race, especially amongst economics
> you get the investment banking internship and all this
> stuff...*

Having given the matter further thought Adrian changed his mind about taking these internships, and again expressed criticisms of his fellow Economics students and their motivations, which he felt were primarily around amassing personal wealth rather than doing something socially useful. His bigger principles about the purpose and value of work came through in his comments:

> *I just got so sick of all the....because the only reason
> anyone does Economics is to get on to those schemes,
> and I withdrew all my applications after getting fed
> up with everything there and looked into kind of
> companies that I thought 'what would I want, if I
> was going to do something that I would enjoy doing
> every day what would it be' and that was kind of
> where I thought about the music route, not directly
> kind of music industry related but something like
> Spotify, a company who are kind of open source
> access to music... I think that's really important. And
> then again....I don't know, how useful that is as a
> job in the grand scheme of things?*

Perhaps more than the other three young men featured in this chapter, Adrian emphasized the need to align career and family ambitions, like some of the young women discussed in subsequent chapters:

> *I guess I'd hope by the time I had kids I'd been...*
> *doing something I was really enjoying, and that it*
> *would be in a company that values kind of their*
> *employees having a life. So hopefully it would just be*
> *a natural kind of slight lull in terms of career focus,*
> *and that then obviously as they get older and go off*
> *to university you kind of maybe get back into it. I*
> *don't want to be coming home at 8 or 9 o'clock at*
> *night and not seeing your kids and then maybe*
> *having a few hours at the weekend, I definitely don't*
> *want that sort of life. I don't think I had that when I*
> *was younger, I think my parents were at home quite*
> *a lot, and I know speaking to people who it seems to*
> *have really affected them that they didn't see their*
> *parents very much when they were younger, and I*
> *definitely don't want to be in that sort of situation. It*
> *would be...staying and trying to do the best at what I*
> *can do in my career, but also at the same time*
> *making sure that I do the best in home.*

Adrian was successful in securing Master's study in Denmark and was seeking to move there straight after graduation when we spoke with him at the end of his undergraduate course, in order to settle before his Master's began. He considered getting postgraduate qualifications the best chance to advance his career and achieve a position where he could do something socially useful. Part of his rationale for choosing to study overseas was that the course was effectively free, unlike in the United Kingdom, and that he could get financial support to study. He contrasted this to the situation in Britain, where, given large numbers of graduates, a postgraduate award would differentiate someone like him from the wider pool and offer a chance for social mobility. However, the cost of postgraduate study effectively meant that only the already well-off could afford it.

When we next spoke with Adrian in 2015 he was part-way through his Master's degree in Denmark and had applied for a PhD course, which he could study whilst working at a bank – his research was on household finance during times of economic recession, so something he felt aligned with his socially conscious values. Adrian was successful in his PhD application and enjoying his time studying. He had spent time in the United States during his postgraduate studies, but was now sure he would rather live in mainland Europe. He was mulling an academic career at a later meeting, but was unsure just where he might want to live and work in the longer term:

> *I want to move somewhere near and then I'll pick a job based on where I choose I guess, or some combination of wherever there's an exciting job or where I want to live...I mean...if I could get a good post-doctoral position I would take it, so that would also be an interesting job. But it's going to be difficult because it's never going to be as comfortable as doing a post-doc here in Denmark, financially or workload wise. And then I have a feeling I don't have enough of a desire academically speaking, so it might be too difficult. Otherwise, I don't know, if I can get a position within a bank where I can run some of my own projects because it turns out that banks are pretty interested in the stuff that I do, then that would also be exciting. Otherwise maybe a smaller company. Basically...I want to have a bit more freedom, so a job that is exciting for me is having freedom.*

Adrian was still committed to what he considered socially useful work, rather than pursuing a career for primarily financial gain. He was contemplating working in the developing world in the future, or in a socially useful financial company in the United Kingdom or Europe:

> *I think if I have a successful company that people use then I imagine I'd feel like I've made a social contribution...if I'm attacking some issue that people have day to day, whether that be in a developing country or in the Western world...I would see that as some sort of contribution socially for the good*

In autumn 2021 Adrian was an academic still working overseas as a post-doctoral researcher after completing his PhD a few years previously. Adrian didn't come from a wealthy background, but he was economically comfortable enough to not be driven by a need to be financially secure to the same extent as some of the working-class participants discussed in Chapters 5 and 6, nor did he see earning money as a marker of masculine success like Dylan. Adrian had been influenced by his parents' strong political worldview and sought socially responsible worthwhile employment, through hard work and academic success.

DYLAN: 'I'VE ALWAYS BEEN DRIVEN BY SUCCESS'

Dylan's parents were both retired business people, although his father worked in a consultancy role 'to prevent himself getting bored'. From the opening exchanges of the first interview we had with Dylan, who was at UWE, his drive and determination to be 'successful' shone clearly. And his definition of success, in marked contrast to both Lloyd and

Adrian, was clear – to be rich, and he saw studying Politics as a good way to achieve that:

> *I just think I've always been quite driven by like success and like my Dad did well in business...so I always wanted to kind of emulate that really – well I don't feel like I need to compete with him but I always wanted to kind of do well really, like I'm quite success driven, money driven I suppose some people would call it, but yeah I'm prepared to work hard for...I'll put in the hours to earn a lot of money. I want a good career really, and I thought that Politics is something that is a good degree, it's not like a namby-pamby degree that I think some people seem to take. And I don't know, I just thought it fitted quite well and I can use it, I can take it on to maybe do a Law conversion and then go to Bar School... But at the moment, yeah, it was just something that I thought I could fit into a career and try and go quite far with it hopefully.*

Dylan's mother had taken a Business Studies degree in her mid-20s, but his father had not attended university, rather he 'started as an apprentice and worked up really basically right from the bottom to like the President of Europe in the company, so he did it the old school way'. His mother had 'worked for about two years' before quitting to look after Dylan and had not worked since. When we first met Dylan he was unsure about whether he would like to work in finance in the City, or be a barrister. Even at the start of his first year Dylan had secured a future internship in a large international investment bank through a friend of his father who was head of the internship scheme there. Unlike Lloyd and particularly Adrian, Dylan did not have to take part-time employment whilst at university 'I've never really had to work...my Mum and Dad would always pay for stuff I wanted to do'.

When we spoke with Dylan at the end of his second year, he was torn between three possible career routes, a Law conversion course followed by bar exams to become a barrister, share and stock trading or brokering, or an internship at an investment bank. His choices were framed to an extent by the fact his parents lived near London and were well connected in those circles. He had access to two of the highly competitive and sought-after investment bank internships through his parents' acquaintances, while their neighbour was a barrister who had promised to help him into the career if that's what he decided to do. Dylan's parents were also wealthy and were keen to support his aspirations. His father had agreed to go into a joint share ownership arrangement with him. Dylan also considered himself quite entrepreneurial, enjoying 'wheeling and dealing' and looking for ways to make money – he said he was 'obsessed' by the 'thrill of chasing money':

> *I like starting little money-making schemes and stuff, and I've always kind of done that as a kid, you know in summers and Christmas, like buying and selling stuff and whatever. And I've got a few like projects....well they're kind of on the back burner while I'm at uni, but like websites and stuff that I'm looking to start. And like that's something that I'm kind of interested in, and I'm probably going to have some time out after uni and I just want to do it just for the experience of starting up, registering a company, being my own boss... and if something came of it then brilliant...hopefully we'll start the next Facebook!*

By his final year Dylan had decided against trying to become a barrister, deciding it was too competitive (as did

Francesca who features in Chapter 4 and Kyle in Chapter 5), and was looking specifically at either foreign exchange trading (for which he was seeking internships), or the entrepreneurial business self-starting route he had mentioned previously. In terms of the foreign exchange trading he was pulling in all the favours he could through his family connections and also planning to move back home to his parents' house due to its relative proximity to London's financial district. Once again he was enjoying access to advantages that relatively few of his peers had:

> *I'm going to go home I think, because we live quite near central London, so kind of what I want to get into is centred in London, so it's really quick to get to, like Canary Wharf and the financial district. So it just makes sense to go home really, and it means I can live at home and not have to pay rent.*

Dylan told us his parents 'own quite a few flats' in London which he could use, but he preferred to move back to their house after graduation. He had investigated starting a tech firm aiming at political advertizing to engage young people, but that didn't take off despite having 'met with some MPs'. Later he took a role with a brokerage selling investments in precious metals and then moved to a foreign currency trading company, a job he had partly acquired through family contacts. He was in a brokering role when we spoke and had ambitions to become a dealer and then a trader, slightly different roles carrying increasing levels of status and reward. Dylan also suggested he still fancied creating a financial services technology start-up firm and was continually working on possible ideas.

When we last heard from Dylan in autumn 2021, he was living with his long-term partner in their own property close to his family. He was a senior treasury manager for a finance company and earning over £100,000. Dylan epitomized the form of masculinity whereby success is measured by wealth (Ingram & Waller, 2015), and he seemed desperate to be seen as successful in the eyes of his father in particular.

SEBASTIAN: A 'HIPPY MUSICIAN IN CORPORATE CLOTHING'?

Whilst Dylan's family were probably the wealthiest of the four young men in this chapter, which afforded him various advantages both whilst at university and following gradua-tion, Sebastian's probably had the highest levels of upper-middle-class social capital. In his own words he had had 'a very, very incredibly middle-class upbringing', having attended a preparatory school, then an independent school as a boarder. Sebastian's father was a partner in a law firm, and his mother a teacher, and both had gone to university them-selves, his father to Cambridge following his own experience at an elite boarding school in London. He said his parents were both 'very, very cultured': 'they've definitely tried to pass it on to me which is why I'm sort of interested in Indian classical music and going off to study that and things, just really oddball things'. They had, for instance, encouraged both Sebastian and his younger sister to study music when young and supported them in their sporting interests too.

Sebastian, who studied Geography at UoB had set himself very high standards academically. In the opening few minutes of his first interview he suggested as follows:

> *If something had gone horribly wrong in my exams and I got 3 Bs – which still like wouldn't be terrible – then I'd probably want to sort of re-take... because I*

wouldn't want to be on a course which was only 3 Bs
requirements I think, to be honest.

Sebastian was a highly accomplished musician, who taught guitar and other stringed instruments as a way of paying his way through university. He was also paid to play gigs and as a session musician in a recording studio, and he funded a trip to India to study the sitar. He had contemplated a career in music after graduation, but was also considering training as a management consultant for a major commercial services company when we spoke with him in his second and third years at university, largely since it was more secure employment. He also felt that, as someone who loved music, he didn't want to tarnish or taint his enjoyment of it by having the pressure of needing to earn a full-time living through it:

> *I do want to earn some money and it's a very risky*
> *career move. I don't want to get bitter about music or*
> *feel I have to do something like, I mean teaching is*
> *fun just because I really believe in what I am doing.*
> *Like I want to pass on the skill that has sort of given*
> *me so much. That's the only sort of cross over*
> *between sort of a commercial aspect of music that I*
> *do. Like I quite like being completely free, being able*
> *to play the music I want to and not sort of feel I have*
> *to do anything which is nice.*

Sebastian liked the idea of travelling for work, especially overseas, and applied for graduate roles with several management consultancy firms with that particular focus in mind. He also applied for the Foreign Office and the wider Civil Service, and hadn't ruled out taking a Master's degree in a few years' time. As a student, Sebastian had also been involved in promoting music and other events, including the Fresher's Ball in his old hall of residence.

In terms of how he felt he had changed since coming to university, at the end of his second year, Sebastian felt he was 'less driven'. He also reflected upon his choice of degree subject:

> *Most people they come to a good university and they are surrounded by people who often are quite driven and they kind of get caught up in that. I'd say definitely I've got less driven. I never was really driven but I always worked hard in school, like I always assumed I wanted to get a really good job and earn lots of money. I nearly chose Engineering or Law as a degree but I kind of worried that if I didn't like it then I would drop out and try and do music as my job, which is probably not a good idea for the reasons I said earlier. So I chose Geography 'cos it's interesting and whatever anyone says about degrees, it's not as hard as Engineering or something and it's part of the reason I chose it. Since then I've realized that I'd be happier if I have a job I enjoy more rather than something that would pay loads more and then like have time for other interests and things as well... I still want to do well, I'll still work hard for things but I'm less driven than before I came to university I think, which most people wouldn't say.*

By the end of his third year at university in 2013 Sebastian had secured a competitive graduate role as a risk analyst with a prestigious international financial services company, based in their Bristol office, but with the expectation of extensive travel both in the United Kingdom and overseas. He had qualms about whether this would suit him in the long term, but felt it would offer additional professional training and valuable skills and experiences for his CV, although he was wary of what he called 'the corporate world'. This was a theme that was revisited repeatedly in later interviews after he had started the job. In the short term, though, he felt this had the advantage of letting him see up close how various businesses worked, which would help him as he finally settled upon a career:

> And so after a couple of years I'll know a lot about how other businesses work because I'll have sort of seen them from the inside... I reckon after a few years I might have a better idea of what I might actually want to do. And it might be this, I might find this really interesting, but it's sort of a good starting point I think.

Sebastian had considered trying to 'make it' as a musician for a few years after graduation, including moving to London to help him do so. However, he decided that if he did it would be much more difficult to subsequently enter 'the corporate world' a few years later, when he would be competing for those prestigious career opportunities against more recent graduates. Some of these would doubtless have undertaken a number of relevant internships, whereas Sebastian had tended to spend his summers travelling and playing (or studying) music. He also felt that there was an expectation on him from others to at least try 'corporate life':

> The school I went to, and my Dad being a lawyer and stuff, it sort of....they don't push me towards it but there's sort of an expectation in the back of your mind that you should try a sort of corporate office job type of thing for a bit at least. And I saw a good opportunity and so I thought I'd go for it. I didn't really expect to get it, but like when I did I was like 'well I can't really turn this down, I've got to try it for a few years at least'. So I don't know, if I like it I can

*stay there, it's a very, very open position so I can
probably....I can find out what I want to do
afterwards. If I like it I could stay for a long time, if I
don't, I've got money and a good CV and can leave
and do music or something like that.*

When we next spoke to Sebastian he had been out of
university for a few years and was still working for the same
global financial services corporation. He reflected favourably
on his decision to do so rather than try to pursue a career in
his 'passion' of music, since he had decided 'I'm just going to
keep it (music) as my thing'. He did consider working for a
socially valuable non-profit organization in the future, if needs
be in a voluntary manner, something he could fund through
teaching or playing his guitar. He suggested:

*I kind of realized it makes purely more sense to get
like a proper job that looks really good on your CV
for a few years first, and then do all the idealistic stuff
later.*

Sebastian also talked of how he used his music to 'de-
corporatize' when not actually working, and that it remained
still 'a really, really big thing' in his life. He was earning
£32,000 two years after starting his job on £22,000, but felt
somewhat personally compromised by that and by the future
structured pay rises he could expect in the next few years, in
terms of the social value of his job:

*You can progress very rapidly, like you have to take
on quite a bit of responsibility each year. But it's
strange, like I definitely do not deserve this salary,
like my expertise or working hours or what I can
contribute in a kind of wider sense, in terms of the
kind of flows in what the company deals with, like
we're definitely worth this much but in terms of kind*

> *of this comparable to other jobs and what my friends*
> *are doing, or the level of expertise they have to*
> *have....a lot of my friends are doing PhDs and I*
> *guess it is really ridiculous I get paid this much, like*
> *it's definitely unfair on virtually every level!*

Sebastian had an interesting approach to work, essentially seeking to become very good and efficient at it, not so he could progress career-wise, but in order to enjoy more free time to escape from what he referred to as 'office life':

> *I kind of realized that I don't like sitting in back*
> *offices doing boring stuff and I like to minimize that*
> *time, so I worked really, really hard to kind of build*
> *skills to make me work faster. So I think I've got*
> *really, really efficient at working...I think I'm the*
> *quickest to get all my work done in the department,*
> *which I've worked really hard to do. Like I quite*
> *enjoy the kind of strategic working out who cares*
> *about what. Like there are a lot of people who will*
> *just do every last detail, and again not having like a*
> *moral feeling for what you're doing and not really*
> *caring. Like I work hard for my colleagues and not*
> *let them down and, you know if there's a good*
> *manager I'll work hard for them...I don't believe in*
> *what I'm doing, so I don't need to do this stuff to the*
> *best of my ability. So I'd say I was probably only*
> *doing 6 hours a day for most of last year, which*
> *probably would have been more like 9 given the*
> *work balance, like that would probably be typical ...*
> *again that's partly like, if you're doing 9 hour days*
> *that would start to get to you, if you're doing 6 then*
> *it's very easy to have a kind of several hour stretch to*
> *'de-corporatize', do music. So I've really tried to do*
> *that.*

Whilst Sebastian enjoyed travelling with his work, he found it was exacting too heavy a price, working full days, travelling on trains and living in hotels around the United Kingdom:

> *I mean you're not really working 24 hours but you're on your own in a city and you don't know anyone, so that's when you realize that it can start to get inside you and that, yeah, you realize if you were doing that for months it would sort of start to change you a bit. So...I started to push back and said like I'm not spending my 20s in back offices doing IT controls and then going back to business hotels...That's when you get home and you haven't got the energy left to do fun stuff. Like I've not struggled with spending my evenings really well, again I've tried to make a point of doing that so the corporate thing feels like a sort of weird thing I do for a couple of years, rather than my main thing.*

At the next interview in 2016 Sebastian was still working for the same firm, but had suffered from tendonitis meaning he had had to significantly scale-back playing music. He had also reduced his scheduled working hours to work two weeks in three and was being paid proportionately less accordingly. He was using his non-working time to develop ideas for helping international development charities, and encouraging social impact and corporate responsibility in large firms. He was working directly with some very senior business people and charity leaders, and really enjoying the voluntary role. He talked of leaving his finance service company and moving into this role in the near future.

The last time we met with Sebastian in the summer of 2017, four years after graduating, he was still at the large corporate firm, earning £39,000 but on a pro-rata basis since he was still working part-time whilst doing voluntary work with the charity sector. He was moving into the field of workplace activism, encouraging people working in big organizations to seek to influence the companies' policies, making them more environmentally friendly, for instance. He was using his professional experiences developed from consulting for large businesses in applying 'hard-headed thinking' to pursue charitable causes and social issues. This, plus his music which he saw as essential to his identity and sense of self, was what Sebastian wanted to spend his foreseeable future doing:

> I hope I'll be a professional workplace activist in the sense that like I'll have moved enough money and changed our systems so that somebody will just fund me to do this on my own terms, which I will be looking to pursue funds for this maybe late this year, early next year. But as things are so unpredictable I have no idea...I will be definitely working the sphere of global justice, hopefully as a systemic activist of some sort.

Sebastian spoke reflectively of his own advantages: '...and again all this like hippy stuff I can only do because I'm like in a situation of middle-class privilege'. But he considered it incumbent upon himself to do what he felt was morally right and to highlight and act upon economic disadvantage nationally and internationally.

By autumn 2021 Sebastian was a self-employed musician, writer and teacher, now living in London, earning 'up to £20,000', the lowest income category of any of our participants. However, he still owned his flat in Bristol which he let out to friends at 'mate's rates'. Sebastian had left the corporate world during the COVID pandemic and was still actively working for social change and to enhance corporate responsibility. He had the capitals to access the corporate world upon graduation, but then chosen to turn his back on it. He did, however, have the financial safety net of a fairly wealthy family and his own property, meaning he could follow his passion of music knowing that financial help was close to hand if necessary.

CONCLUSION

The four middle-class young men in this chapter represent different forms of contemporary masculinities (Ingram & Waller, 2014), yet each is informed by a range of factors, including their classed upbringing and the capitals upon which they could draw. Social class is an incredibly complex issue as explained elsewhere in this book. However, the forms of masculinity displayed by the men in the four narrative accounts highlighted in this chapter are undoubtedly *informed* or otherwise *influenced* by their backgrounds.

Both Dylan and Adrian were interested in a career related to finance, but each approached it from a different starting point and different dispositions, shaped by their different class backgrounds. Adrian wanted to achieve what he considered a socially worthwhile career, doing so through commitment and hard work, in line with classed political values learned from his parents, and not dissimilar to the values demonstrated by Sebastian. Dylan had the self-confidence and sense of entitlement to feel he would be successful at anything he undertook, and his father, with a business background, supported and helped him, utilizing his own economic and social capital. By contrast Adrian and Lloyd had to achieve any goals through their own efforts and abilities; Such dispositions informed both their classed and their gendered identities.

4

SLOW TRAIN TO THE TOP? MIDDLE-CLASS WOMEN'S NARRATIVES OF BUILDING A CAREER

This chapter deals with the experiences of middle-class women graduates. It might be presumed that young women from middle-class backgrounds shared the privileges of their male peers and had similar advantages in the competition for careers. As we shall see, they do share some advantages, in terms of the possession of high levels of economic, social and cultural capitals. However, of the four groups we are studying in this book, middle-class women were the most likely to enter university without a career plan, and, significantly, the most likely to finish their studies with no clear idea of what they wanted to do next. While going to university is absolutely a norm for middle-class girls, their attitudes are less focused on economic outcomes than the other groups. A number told us they intended to return home, get a temporary job or travel and then explore future career possibilities, what participants in the earlier Bristol study *Winners and Losers* referred to as 'sorting my life out'.

We must note that the labour market which our graduates are entering is shaped by gender; men and women tend to do different jobs. Moreover, women enter the labour market on slightly differing terms. First, the labour market remains segregated by gender (and by ethnicity, though that largely falls outside our research). Segregation has two dimensions. Horizontal segregation refers to men and women being clustered into different jobs: men dominate as lorry drivers, mechanics, builders and brain surgeons; women are the majority of secretaries, beauticians, carers and cleaners. Vertical segregation reflects the fact than men are more likely to get promotions: within each industry men occupy more of the posts at the top of the hierarchy. Many factors lie behind these patterns. Some are historical: our occupational structure developed after industrialization, especially during the Victorian era, when women were considered inferior to men and a doctrine of separate spheres was developed. Jobs became labelled as 'men's work' or 'women's work', and the labels have stuck (Bradley, 1989). These shape the expectations of boys and girls through the images they see of adults in books and in the media. By and large, those occupations in which women dominate are seen as less socially valuable and are less well paid.

Since the 1960s, these stereotypes and patterns of difference have been challenged by feminist activists, resulting in legislation designed to tackle sexism and unequal pay. Most large organizations and all public sector organizations now have equal opportunities policies, such as mentoring schemes and programmes to help women and BAME workers into management. Despite this, gender segregation has proved remarkably resistant. Some of this is down to individual choice; but it is also strongly influenced by women's reproductive responsibilities. If children come along, women characteristically have career breaks, many returning to work part-time. Although few of the graduates had children, the future possibility of motherhood clearly affected some young women's choices.

In this chapter we explore how class background and the type of university attended affect these young women's fortunes. We begin with two women, Hannah and Francesca, who come from prosperous families with abundant capitals: we could describe them as 'upper-middle-class'. Their stories are varied, however, by the fact that Hannah went to UoB and Francesca to UWE. The stories show the considerable impact of 'fit' or lack of it. By contrast, Lauren (UoB) and Harriet (UWE) come from more modest backgrounds and might be seen as 'lower-middle-class'. Compared to the working-class women featured in Chapter 6, Lauren and Harriet are able to draw on some capital resources to help them along, but notably less so than Hannah and Francesca. Consequently, it takes them longer to sort out a future that is viable, with less assistance along the way.

'I CAN SEE CLEARLY NOW!' HANNAH'S STORY

I've never considered not going [to university] really. Because it's the natural thing to do. I didn't really feel ready at 18 to go out and start working...I still felt quite young and going into another sort of structured education, even though there's more freedom, that kind of made complete sense because I'm not really ready to go and work yet, and I wasn't sure what I wanted to do.

Hannah's background can be described as comfortable. Both her parents are doctors; an older brother was already at

Bristol University studying for an arts degree and two younger sisters were still at school. Growing up in Sussex, Hannah went to a preparatory school but decided she didn't want to proceed to boarding school. She attended the local grammar school, which appealed to her as it was strong on sports. She took up a place at UoB to read Psychology, but, as the quotation above from her first interview shows, she typified the characteristics of this group, seeing university as a kind of 'natural' life stage but with no clear career plan. HE is seen as a pleasurable transition away from childhood, but there is no urgency about career or employment; tellingly, Hannah spoke of her situation in terms of a 'safety net':

> *You're not really independent yet, so you're in a bit of like a safety net, and you've kind of got everything, not as much as school, but things are still kind of handed to you on a plate. Because you've got enough money; you've got your student loans...it's not really like you're going to struggle.*

Hannah had no worries about money as her parents were paying her fees. She had taken out loans to cover her living costs and her parents helped her with other expenses.

Throughout her undergraduate years, Hannah emphasized her indecisiveness about what she wanted to do, but also speculated that she might choose a conversion course to study medicine. Her choice of psychology was made because she didn't want slavishly to follow in her parents' footsteps, but clearly the idea of becoming a doctor had been in her mind. For example, at school she chose to observe in a hospital as work experience, though it had failed to convince her that this was the career for her:

> *I was doing shadowing of a doctor round, like various doctors for a week in a hospital. So I'd go*

*and sit in their clinics and listen to patients and then
into the theatre watching some operations with an
orthopaedic surgeon...I thought I'd be really
squeamish but it wasn't actually too bad...I didn't
particularly like the atmosphere in the hospital.*

She was well aware of the 'rules of the game' in terms of
building a career. She realized an internship would help, and,
knowing that volunteering would look good on her CV, she
signed up to work on the university helpline. At the end of her
second year she went to Kenya for a month volunteering at an
AIDS project:

*Helping women to kind of get their lives back on
track and helping them with farming and things so
they could look after their children and provide them
with food and stuff. And we went into a clinic as well
for infants, and we were kind of in charge of their
Reception bit, so when they came in we'd like take all
their weights and stuff and their measurements and
temperature, and then we'd send them into the
doctor.*

She also spent a week shadowing a psychiatrist, helping
him administer tests and questionnaires, despite having
decided that jobs in psychology were not really for her.
Significantly, social capital enabled her to set up both these
CV-enhancing activities. Her brother fixed her a contact in
Kenya and she stayed in his house, saving money; while the
psychiatrist was the father of her sister's school friend.

Like many of the graduates in our study, Hannah spoke of
her passion for 'travelling'. We should emphasize that this
meant more than just a holiday in the sun: it involved moving
around, seeing different cultures and places, having adventures, managing the arrangements. Travel figured largely in

her summers: in her first year she went with her family on safari in South Africa, plus a month travelling around Indonesia with a boyfriend. The next year, as well as the Kenya trip, she visited both Majorca and Mexico with her family. Few working-class young adults would have had the capital for such experiences, unless they had found a way to 'work their passage'. Although Hannah took waitressing jobs in the summer to help fund these adventures, she did not take on term-time work and even her waitressing was reflective of her class background: she worked at Wimbledon tennis tournament, catering for company directors, and on another occasion at a mansion belonging to a horse racing magnate:

> He's just ridiculously rich so...he has all these kind of big formal dinners and things, and like parties that he throws. They must cost thousands and thousands of pounds. They need kind of silver service waitresses and waiters, and they're all people from the schools locally...It's quite exciting because it's such a kind of like big glamorous event!

Hannah enjoyed her undergraduate years at UoB. We asked all the students to score their experience out of 10, and Hannah gave it a nine, a higher score than the others discussed in this chapter. She described herself a little confusingly as 'a typical Bristol student' but 'not a typical student'. By this she meant she didn't conform to the popular stereotype of students as drunken party animals going out every night; but she saw herself as similar to her own group of friends: 'I'm probably more, I don't know, on the quieter side'. She described her peers as hard working and competitive, some being more 'driven' than she was. She emphasized how she felt 'at home' in Bristol, that the people there were similar to her friends at home: 'it's sort of a bigger version of where I live'. Her view of the 'typical (University of) Bristol student' was also informed by visiting a boyfriend who was studying Engineering at Coventry and contrasting his experience with hers:

> *I found everyone at Bristol, almost everyone, my friends anyway, were all really driven with work and quite determined to do well. Whereas I think quite a lot of them (at Coventry) are happy...they're just content to do a bit less.*

Though she did not express it in these terms, it was clear that there was a class fit, which we will see was missing in the case of Francesca at UWE. 'There isn't much diversity', she commented.

Ending with a very high 2.1, Hannah had decided by the third year that she did want to pursue a career in medicine. She ended up accepting a place to study an undergraduate degree in medicine at UoB where she was happy to stay. She could do this because her parents continued to pay her fees, though she became more committed to finding temporary work to contribute to the costs.

We caught up with her at the end of her first year as a medical student. She was highly engaged with her course, finding elements of it challenging, but working very hard and scoring high marks. By the second year she was living in a fashionable area in a small flat with her new boyfriend, who was training in accountancy. At the final interview she was still enjoying the course but not yet sure what route to follow in her career

> *I've pretty much ruled out surgery just from experience. I just think I'd be more suited to medicine which is more clinics and thinking about what medication people need and managing their care that way... I'm sort of considering maybe paediatrics, maybe being a GP, maybe psychiatry.*

Hannah is well aware that she is lucky to be able to follow this path because of the continued support, emotional, cultural and financial, from her parents:

> *It's a huge amount of support, they're so supportive of me doing this degree and they're so encouraging and so generous in how they're supporting me with it. And I think that also the fact that they're both doctors means they can relate to it.*

The support has also helped her to indulge her passion for travelling, which is clearly shared by her parents. She describes her family as very oriented to Europe (Brexit was a horrible shock to them) but they also undertake more adventurous journeys. For example, after her second year as a medical student, there was a family holiday in Sri Lanka, followed by backpacking in India, and at the time of her final interview she explained:

> *I love going home, and we're all going on holiday end of August, even my Brother who is 26, and we love having that time together. We're a very close family. We're going to Corsica.*

We have described Hannah's background as 'upper-middle-class', and her story has made clear that the family possesses ample supplies of economic, social and cultural capital. However, to make the point about the gradations within the middle-class, it is worth mentioning that at UoB Hannah encountered people whom she considered more wealthy and privileged than herself. Her account, however, involves a recognition of her 'luck' at her own privileged situation:

> *I have certain friends who have to work the whole time whilst being at Bristol to fund it and other friends who have come from boarding school and*

*seem to have unlimited money to spend. There's
quite a few students that seem to have kind of second
homes that they'll go off to for the weekend and
homes abroad that they'll go to. And I've got friends
here sometimes that I know are really lucky and well
off and say things like 'I'm so poor at the moment'
and it really irritates me because like that's just not
true. Because actually I am quite aware of the
differences, I really appreciate that I'm actually quite
lucky.*

Hannah's experiences, then, are clearly shaped by her class background. Her capitals, both inherited and acquired, have guided her towards a prestigious rewarded professional future. Her caution in making her final choice was facilitated by her parents' financial situation and clearly influenced by the family milieu (her younger sister was also studying medicine by then). We were impressed, however, by her acknowledgement of her privileged position, described as 'luck' and by her thoughtfulness in choosing a career which would bring her equivalent stability and security; and also which would, in her view, enable her to combine having children and a career, as her mother had done:

*I think that's a really important part of life, having
children, and I really hope to some day, so if it meant
taking maternity leave or time out of work then I
would definitely want to do that. But having said
that, I had a nanny growing up and I still saw plenty
of my Mum, even though she had a full-time job as a
GP, so she was perfectly able to balance it.... I'm
aiming to have a career that I'm not going to lose by
having children.*

In 2021, Hannah was working in obstetrics in a hospital in New Zealand, where her fiancé had gained a diplomatic post, and they owned a property. Her story exemplifies middle-class social reproduction.

FRANCESCA'S STORY: OVERCOMING DISAPPOINTMENTS

Francesca, who studied Law at UWE, makes an interesting comparison with Hannah. She comes from a similarly comfortable background: her parents both worked as successful public sector administrators, and her father then became a professor at an RG university. Like Hannah's parents they possess considerable amounts of valuable economic, cultural and social capital. They own a flat in Paris, which they frequently visit, and both speak French fluently, passing on this skill to Francesca through French lessons as a child.

Francesca told us how she decided when a teenager that she would like to become a lawyer:

> *My parents took me to see Michael Mansfield, he's quite a famous barrister, and went to see to him and then afterwards went up to speak to him....He was so enthusiastic about what he did and sort of the issues that he worked with, and that's something I'm interested in.*

She drew on social capital to secure several placements to learn more about the legal profession:

> *Well the first one I did in the Crown Court, so that was quite an easy one to get because they're really open about it. The second one, one of my best friends, her dad's a lawyer in London so I managed*

to get a placement with him. And then I did another
one last holiday with a family friend who is also a
lawyer in London.

Her family were able to help her in selecting universities and courses:

If I needed questions I knew that they were good
people to ask because my Dad worked in it and my
Mum did a lot with my Brother when he applied.
And I asked my Brother for help as well.

Despite these advantages, Francesca's plans suffered a setback when she failed to get her expected grades at A level, to the surprise of her teachers *and* parents. She could not attend the universities she had hoped for; instead, following discussion with her father, she went through clearing to secure a place at UWE. When we interviewed her in the first year, she was making the best of things. She praised the teaching and the staff at UWE, stating that she didn't think it would have been better elsewhere. However, in subsequent interviews, she expressed a more jaded view of studying at UWE, mainly because of her feeling of being different from most of the students there:

A lot of people I spoke to were doing the subject just
because they didn't really know what else to do,
which I thought was a bit of an odd reason to do a
fairly hard degree. I have quite fixed ideas of what I
want to do and a lot of people were....not
unmotivated but they didn't really know what they
wanted to do, and I guess, yeah there were some
quite unmotivated people and that sort of frustrates
me quite a lot.

Many UWE students, especially those from working-class backgrounds, have to take on term-time work, and are thus inhibited from pursuing extra-curricular activities, unlike Francesca, who has strong sporting interests. In her home town, the whole family had joined a sports club: Francesca was coached in various sports and played two at junior county level. She also played the cello in the county youth orchestra. On joining the orchestra at UWE, she was dismayed to find that most of its members were not students but staff or alumni. She identified a cultural gap between her and many of her fellow students:

> *There's no demand at UWE to do a course where it takes you abroad in a non-English speaking country. There's no opportunity in Law to go to a place that speaks French or Italian.*

All this contrasted with her life back at home:

> *Everyone I hung around with at school and most of my close friends, we all were going into like a vocational course and to do something we've really wanted to do for a long time. We've got ideas of where we want to go and we all have really similar interests, like political opinion and things like that... Whereas here it's one big group of people again but I feel quite different from them.*

Francesca lived in a middle-class part of her home town, attended a high-performing local state school which was located close to a private school and had friends from both. She came, as did many participants, from a class homogenous background into a more mixed environment where she felt uneasy. In addition as a late entrant she did not gain a place in UWE's popular student village, but had to live in the UNITE student accommodation in the centre of Bristol. She expressed envy of the lifestyle of friends she visited at Russell Group universities and made attempts to transfer to higher-status universities, but her applications failed. She tried to make the best of things, despite periodic feelings of homesickness and regret, but throughout her stay appeared oriented to her friends 'back home':

> *The friends I've been friends with for the longest time in my life, and then friends that I've known who are now at university there, it's a good chance to go and see them. I just really enjoy going back. I do miss it.*

Just as many working-class students struggle with 'lack of fit' at elite universities, it is clear that, although she did not express it in these terms, Francesca experienced a lack of class fit at UWE. To compensate for negative feelings she indulged in what in an earlier publication we described as 'hyper-mobilization of capitals' (Bathmaker et al., 2016), captaining her sports team for two years, winning tournaments, playing in the orchestra and acting as course rep. This enhanced her CV, along with the legal placements she undertook each summer, including one at an elite City of London firm. Her class background aided her in all this, as she was helped financially by her parents:

> *My parents pay for the fees and I took the student loan out for covering accommodation and living expenses, but I get an allowance from my parents every month. Then books and sort of trips and stuff are paid for as well. And every year me and my parents talk about how much I need for everything. They pay for my bus and all my sports fees and everything. Yeah, and orchestra, it sort of mounts up when you have to do all the membership fees and buy*

the kit and stuff like that, and renting out courts and
buying gym pass. So I'm really grateful for that.

Despite the considerable amounts of economic, social and
cultural capital, however, the impact of attending a new university had a strong impact on Francesca's future career. She
repeatedly told us of her desire to become a barrister:

I came to uni wanting to do a bar course which is like
the barristers' qualification and I still really, really
want to do that…but I've become more attracted to
other things, like working in-house, so rather than
being independent and self-employed which is what
most of them are, like working as an in-house
barrister which is like in the company, like Shell and
BP have their own lawyers.

During her third year Francesca applied for a scholarship
to cover the costs of a bar course, which in London costs
£15,000, but did not succeed in gaining one. What she told us
about her experiences and the requirements for joining the bar
were quite startling and explain *precisely* why it is fairly
impossible for working-class candidates to enter this elite
profession, which appears almost medieval in its customs and
practices. First one must choose to join one of the four historical Inns of Court and learn to socialize with barristers and
judges:

There are all sorts of traditions. Before you can
qualify as a barrister you have to have sat 14 dinners
at your Inn and have had to go to certain speeches
and training sessions… be accepted to go to this
dinner and you meet current members, and meet the
Head of the Inn and have lectures about joining in.

The Inns are fussy about Master's qualifications, some requiring them and some not, which needs careful research. After the bar course and a possible Master's, applicants must join in the competition for a pupillage. They are permitted to apply five times, before a final rejection. The years of rejection may be used to acquire relevant experience and jobs, meaning that new graduates are in competition with older candidates.

It was not entirely clear why failing to get the scholarship led Francesca to abandon her long-standing ambition to be a barrister. Perhaps she found the completion too daunting: only about 1 in 40 applicants got the award. The fact that the other candidates were older than herself and most had Oxbridge degrees certainly struck her. Although the recruiters had told her that going to UWE would not affect her chances, she was (rightly we suspect) unconvinced:

> *But the fact is, when you look on everyone's CVs online, because they're all published at the Chambers ...everyone has gone to either Oxford or Cambridge, a couple from sort of Bristol and Durham – or incredibly good foreign universities like the Sorbonne in Paris or Harvard or Yale.*

Despite this setback, Francesca landed on her feet. The previous summer, she had taken an unpaid internship with an insurance company in Australia. Once again, her parents provided economic backup, paying for the travel and living expenses. Francesca worked for the in-house legal team and was taken under the wing of her section head, dealing with insurance and risk issues.

This experience was to prove helpful when she graduated. She applied for a number of graduate schemes, while working in a restaurant to earn money. She secured a job in a company in her home town, but was then invited to apply to an insurance company for a graduate scheme, which was where she was working when we caught up with her. She was one of four candidates chosen from a field of 450: it was a full-time post paying £30,000, and it involved the use of her legal knowledge:

> *I do a lot of work with contracts and agreements, so that definitely helps you understand the terminology, like legal terminology and how to approach lawyers and what sort of things they want to hear, what they don't want to hear. I get a lot of training as well, and we get two weeks with a law firm...the lawyers instruct, we work alongside them.*

With vague thoughts of returning to the law later in life, at her final interview, Francesca was happy and settled, living in a flat in London, earning enough to have overseas holidays, still with her boyfriend from UWE and enjoying her social life. By 2021, she was engaged, owned a property with her fiancé having moved back to her home town, and had risen to a management role.

Despite early disappointments, Francesca had used capitals inherited from her parents plus her acquired assets to play the game successfully and manoeuvre herself into a good place in the graduate labour market. Her story also illustrates, however, how tightly controlled is entry into the top echelons of the legal profession; very few working-class candidates would be able take on the formidable hurdles and costs required to become a barrister.

HARRIET'S STORY: YOU CAN MAKE IT IF YOU TRY

Throughout this book we have been arguing that the broad terms 'middle-class' and 'working-class' conceal many shades of subtle difference. Nurses and supervisors, for example, are categorized as middle-class but their share of capital resources are very different from those of, say, top business executives or professionals such as lawyers and doctors. Indeed, such people have been described as constituting an intermediate class or as being 'semi-professionals'. So far in this chapter, we have explored the experiences of two young women from prosperous professional families. Our next two graduates come from less wealthy backgrounds and thus have fewer capitals upon which to draw.

Harriet, an English student at UWE, described herself as 'at the low end of the middle-class'. Her father had been a mature student and was now a primary school head; her mother had dropped out from university and was a part-time NHS administrator. Harriet had three brothers, two of whom were studying medicine. Harriet described their house in South London as small and crowded, and it was evident from her story that the family, though close and loving, were not very wealthy. Harriet's experience of university was different from those of Hannah and Francesca because of this lack of economic capital. But the interest of her story is the use she made of her more limited resources to move towards her goals.

Harriet attended local schools, first a comprehensive, next an all girls' school, and then a college. Although a bright and book-loving child, she never quite seemed to reach her educational aspirations: her A levels were not as good as she had hoped. One teacher summed up:

> *My teacher just looked at me and was like 'Harriet, I know you're very clever but how can you get the best mark in the class and the worst mark in the class'.*

Similarly, she was to underachieve at UWE, where she aimed for a 2.1 but ended with a 2.2. Although she was quite critical of some of the teaching, and felt it was old fashioned compared to courses taken by others at UWE, she also put this down to her own lack of focus and a feeling of not being clear what she wanted from the future. She had struggled with choice of subjects and, like many of our female participants, had no definite career in mind. In fact, her approach to university was very similar to Hannah's as she saw it in terms of a sheltered passage to maturity:

> *I always knew that I was going to go to uni, I didn't want to miss out on the whole experience of like growing up.... Moving out for the first time but it's kind of in a structured environment I guess, it's kind of like a little stepping stone, you learn how to... like look after yourself a bit more.*

Harriet was clear that she did not want to teach (a destination for many of our less well-off female graduates). She chose English because she had enjoyed writing stories as a child, and the idea of getting into publishing or journalism was something she developed as she proceeded through her degree:

> *At the moment I'm thinking about going into publishing....I've been trying to look for something because I felt when I lose motivation of work it's because I'm like "what's the point"... There's a society of young publishers and stuff, because I don't really know enough about the work, there's a lot of work experience you have to do for it. And they send you newsletters and stuff and everything I've been reading. I've been like "yeah, this sounds like something I'd want to do".*

Another factor was her need to earn money to help herself through university, given her family's situation of having to support three students at once, and her brothers' medical degrees involving five years of study. Harriet took a gap year and worked at a bank, which enabled her to amass savings. In Bristol, she worked in a supermarket on the till for two days a week, which covered half her rent to save her parents expense. But, as with the working-class students who had to take jobs, this encroached on her time and was frustrating:

> *Struggling so much this term, it would be nice to just have enough to go out when I want or....buy some new shoes when I want, you know, every so often. And even just to start saving a little bit again, even if it was just like £50 a month.*

In contrast to many of our middle-class students, Harriet was unable to 'go travelling' in the summer vacation: instead she extended her job to full-time to save up for the next year. She often spoke of being tired and needing a holiday, but those she took were short seaside trips, not the adventures to Australia, Thailand and India enjoyed by Hannah and Francesca. Once again, she was hampered by the lack of economic capital:

> *I went to Barcelona for a week so that was good, but nothing too adventurous I guess. With my boyfriend, yeah...we wanted to go away for longer but it's kind of money, money stops everything I guess at the moment.*

However, her family did provide her with some cultural and social capital as she sought to plan for her future. She told us that she often chatted to her father about her essays and drew on a contact of her mother for advice on publishing:

> *I've got a family friend whose daughter, her dad though is like a CEO of a publishing house or*

something, so I was like 'oh, I'll go and see him over the summer'.

Although Harriet had arrived at university lacking a clear idea of her future, she was aware of the need to develop a strategy for getting a job. She talked about the need to plan, to research out possibilities, especially as the areas she had identified as being of interest to her were highly competitive, and involved having to start out as an unpaid worker. She was as aware as Hannah and Francesca of the 'rules of the game' but lacked the economic resources to participate fully. For example, she knew it would be useful to gain some work experience on a placement in the summer of her second year but felt it necessary to go on working: 'I wish I could have done that but yeah, kind of reality, I have to earn some money'. Working in term time and holidays hampered her ability to build her CV as Hannah and Francesca had done, but she had taken up a sport, partly to maintain her fitness, and in her second year had become president of the society. Looking back later, she felt that she had been more involved with the sports scene at UWE than with her English course.

Harriet described herself as a 'home-bird' and like Francesca she seemed to find it difficult to settle at UWE. There were difficulties with housemates, a best friend quit because of depression and she missed her family and friends:

> *When you're just a bit homesick you can't really like talk to people as much here. Like they don't get you quite as much as some people at home, like my best friends at home who have known me for ever, so I just make sure I call them up. Skype's good because you can see them face to face.*

Harriet described herself as depressed and demotivated by her final year, and this seems to have impacted on her exam performance. She spoke of her father helping her through, but she struggled with her anxieties about money and her lack of a goal: she envied her brothers having a clear pathway with their medical degrees. She was not unusual in this: many of our participants confessed to feelings of anxiety about their future, and the career uncertainty of so many of the middle-class young women may have made them particularly vulnerable to such feelings.

Given this, we expected Harriet would return home after graduating, but in fact she stayed in Bristol, rented a flat and got herself a job in a marketing company. She also had a new boyfriend who was living with his parents while completing a Master's in Finance. She described the routine they had constructed, which may have helped to improve her mental well-being:

> *He's just got a new job in finance but before he was working at a sports centre. So he worked various jobs during uni like lifeguard and he did like sales and marketing. So we got into quite a routine, especially week nights, not so much like a Friday, but walking over after work, going to the gym and by the time that's done he's finished, I can see him then.*

This continuing relationship proved to be the turning point in her life, enabling her to think more positively about her future prospects. When we next caught up with her, she had quit her job and moved back to her parents' home in London, but was putting into action her plans to move into journalism, applying for work experience in the field.

Now having a clear goal, Harriet pursued strategies to achieve it and was rewarded with some success. She had joined an organization which aimed to help young people into media jobs. Their website offered clips on how to construct CVs, details of internships and advertized events:

I've been to a couple of networking events in London with other people who work in journalism, so that was quite good. I've been trying to blog more, so like you know practice my writing. I've actually been offered some online work experience, just a couple of pieces. It was a magazine company....I met someone at one of the networking events and sort of followed up with an email. They said 'if you have any ideas for the online site we'll happily put them up with your by-line', to start, you know, begin loading a portfolio with my name to it. So yeah in the last week I sent over some ideas, they came back and said 'oh yeah these two are great'.

Harriet described herself as having been quite shy when younger, but her experiences at work (she had gained promotion in her marketing job, which had helped her develop her writing skills) had boosted her confidence. Like Francesca, she had not been totally happy during her time at UWE, but had compensated by her sporting involvement. This heightened confidence had motivated her to attend a 'speed-dating' event sponsored by the magazine company:

It was like 6 people from the magazine and they had different tables...they grouped you up. it was say like four of you and one person who worked there, and it was just like a 10 minutes on each table just asking questions.

Staying at home enabled her to pursue these strategies to attain a job, as she knew she would need to start off a journalism career with unpaid internships. At the time of her next interview, she was renting a flat with her UWE boyfriend, who was now working in a city firm. She described how she had contributed to their income by temping in an office, while also pursuing freelancing experience. Then she had a stroke of luck, when someone pulled out of an internship working for a media company and they offered her the place. Before that she had done some months with a publishing company, helped by a contact from UWE:

> *I had a friend who worked in publishing and they needed some help, so I actually got a few months' work – so like with big publishers. I was re-writing stuff and lots of research and things, so that's what kind of took up my time over summer to autumn. It was paid, which is amazing. What I'm doing now is only expenses, so you can imagine I'm running dry a bit now. I was really lucky that my friend....I met her in Bristol, her husband was a (sportsman) so I knew him through uni.*

Through this mixture of freelancing, building networks of useful contacts, taking unpaid internships and paid temporary work, Harriet was acquiring relevant experience:

> *Because my magazine's got some freelance writers – you build up your contacts. And I know there are some websites that want content written that you can sign up for, but for like getting in like the main magazines and stuff it's often about emailing like the Editor and saying 'I've got this idea', like pitching an idea. Often people seem to do it in the very first place obviously trying to get a job they'll freelance, once they're quite established it's good because you've got so many contacts that you can make it your living.*

Her strategies paid off! At her final interview, she was living in a new flat with her boyfriend, planning (at last) to go travelling in Greece, and had secured a job as an editorial assistant on a magazine, paying £22,000 a year:

*I was actually quite looking forward to telling you
that because I went 'oh yeah it's gone full circle' so
that's good. I'm still in London, just a bit closer to
where my new job is and so in a nice new apartment
which is lovely.*

Harriet's story, then, is one of determination paying off,
with the aid of a bit of luck. It also built on cultural capital
from her background. After the low point at the end of her
second year, she was able to develop a strategy for working in
a highly competitive field and succeed in getting a job. Her
success depended partly on her own efforts to be financially
independent; and partly on living at home in London for a few
months while she was building up her experience through
internships. She was also able to utilize social capital both
from her family background, from contacts made at UWE and
through her networking strategy, while her boyfriend's earnings allowed her to live in London despite her limited income.
It was no easy ride, as she lacked the more considerable assets
possessed by Hannah and Francesca. Her trajectory, therefore, is closer to that of the young women from working-class
backgrounds explored in Chapter 6. But given the setbacks
she suffered, she used what assets she had to remarkably good
and strategic effect. As she told her interviewer:

*Life's a journey you know, it's not just facing the end
goal, it's nice to look back on it and just see where
I've come from.*

LAUREN'S STORY: 'I JUST WANT TO BE HAPPY'

I've absolutely no idea what I want to do. I don't even have options or anything, it's just blank.

Like Hannah and Harriet, Lauren, who studied Sociology at UoB, started her degree with no idea what career she wanted. But she differed from them in that, at the time when we last interviewed her, she was still undecided and living at home with her mother.

Lauren's mother, a primary school teacher, was divorced from her father: he had remarried and worked overseas. Lauren lived with her mother and sister in a small West Country town. Although when she started her degree her father lived abroad with his wife and two sons, he seemed to have strong influence on Lauren, encouraging her to prosper academically and go to a prestigious university.

Possibly as a result of the family break-up, Lauren's educational history had been disrupted. It took her several years to complete her A levels:

Well I'd missed a lot of school and for the first year my attendance was really low but because I got good grades they let me carry on. And then my attendance kind of got worse… I think other students were complaining about me, like preferential treatment that I had, and in the end they decided to let me go.

Her mother's social capital came to the rescue here, as she was able to find tutors who helped Lauren to complete her studies at home:

She had contacts with some of like the secondary schools in the area……so she either spoke to people

she knew and asked around for them at their school,
or she actually rang the schools direct.

Lauren showed some determination to go to Bristol University, as she persuaded them to lower the grades for her offer. As she told us, 'I didn't really need much advice, I just did it all myself really, like looked on the internet, like sent off for prospectuses and then made my own decision'. She chose Sociology because it appeared interesting, although she had also considered business because of her father's career.

Her mother had helped with providing tutors, but it was clear that she was not particularly well off and Lauren took some pride in being financially competent. She had inherited some money from grandparents, but also had worked in a gift shop before she dropped out of school. As a student, she lived modestly and didn't go out a great deal:

I saved up quite a lot before I went to uni obviously
because I was working part-time for two years...But
I get a bit of money from my Dad each month, and
my Mum gives me a bit of money at the end of term
so I'm doing fine with money...I keep it in a higher
interest account, so it's just having to remember to
transfer it so then I don't go overdrawn.

Lauren described herself as independent and mature, partly as a result of her difficult transition from school. She spoke of enjoying her course – she scored it seven in the final year – but unlike the other three we have discussed, she seemed detached from playing the competitive academic game:

I know I'm capable of getting a first because I've had
a few marks which have been in like the 70s. I think
my Dad's kind of expecting me, he's saying 'oh yeah
a 2:1 is still good', but I think he secretly wants me to
get a first. My Sister got a first for her degree. I don't

*think I've got that kind of motivation to push myself
for a first.*

Lauren appeared somewhat detached from the university experience. Her closest relationship was with her sister, with whom she took holidays. She didn't form a romantic relationship during her degree, telling us she 'didn't want to kiss a lot of frogs'.

After her second year, Lauren got a job in a shop in Bristol, and continued to work there at weekends during term time. Prizing her ability to manage her money, Lauren reflected on the capitals her family could provide and their limitations:

*I think if I was struggling for money they would help
me out financially. They wouldn't just give me a load
of money because that's not like the kind of people
they are. I think after finishing uni, yeah, my Mum
will let me live back home. Like I might have to pay
eventually if I'm just still stuck at home like a year
later, pay like a little bit of rent. I don't think my
Mum really has any contacts. My Dad does but
they're all in kind of sciency fields.*

In fact after her degree she did return to live with her mother, while continuing in her uncertainty about her career:

*I think I have like a weird relationship with the...well
not with the future but the way I see the future...this
sounds really like pessimistic or weird, but I can't see
myself in the future. I try and like think about what
will I be like in like 5 or 10 years and I just...can't
vision anything, I just can't imagine it.*

Her mother turned out after all to have a useful contact, somebody who worked for a local charity, and Lauren worked as an office assistant for her, which she felt would strengthen her CV, but lost the job when her employer was made redundant. Subsequently she found work three days a week at a local café. She enjoyed the relationships with the women who worked there with her, although they were much older, and described how she would go to the pub with them to 'have a laugh and a drink'.

Lauren seemed happy living at home:

> *It's just Mum and I and two cats. And it's fine. I think we've like come up with quite a good kind of balance. So I'm not currently paying any rent, even though she has broached the topic a few times but she just hasn't taken it any further. And I just help out where I can, I'll cook dinners, I'll do her packed lunch for her work and things like that.*

However, she acknowledged that her mother was putting pressure on her to find a 'proper job' while her father favoured her doing a Master's degree.

At her last interview she was once again working as an occasional researcher with her mother's friend, who had set up as a consultant supporting local charities. But there had occurred a crucial incident when she tried to apply for a more formal charity post and described herself as having a 'total meltdown'. Her mother intervened and sent her to the doctor. For the first time she opened up about her mental health problems, panic attacks and depression, which blocked her from moving forward and appeared to have sprung from the family break-up:

> *I feel more positive because I made the step to go to the doctors and I've been referred to another service, and that's going to see them in a couple of weeks or something, there's a waiting list. So I feel more positive that I've made the step to kind of adjust*

these issues in my life which are holding me back, so I
think at the moment I'm seeing the future in terms of
kind of getting myself better.

Lauren was not alone among the young women we interviewed in experiencing mental health issues caused by the
pressures of competition at university and in the labour
market. But what made her stand out from the others, such as
the three discussed earlier, was her resistance to the culture of
aspiration and hyperactivity in which most of our graduates
were caught up. Indeed, we should perhaps admire her
determination to do things her own way. It was indicative that
she rejected the notion of 'travel' so popular among our
middle-class graduates, telling us 'I don't have this big vision
of like travelling round like Asia or whatever. I'd just rather
just go on holiday'.

We can see this as resistance to the culture of achievement
and individual self-realization which has marked out the lives
of young middle-class people in the twenty-first century and a
clinging to older, more solid values. As she told us:

I just want to like whatever I'm doing, I just want to
be happy in it. I see my goal as happiness.

There *is* a happy ending as in 2021 Lauren was living in
Bath with a partner and had a full-time permanent secure job
in the finance sector.

CONCLUSIONS

I had gone there (Paris) immediately after coming
down from Oxford with a lovely, shiny, useless new

*degree, in a faute-de-mieux middle-class way, to fill
in time.*

This was how Margaret Drabble described the heroine of
her first book, *A Summer Birdcage*, written in 1963 soon after
she herself had graduated from Cambridge. In the succeeding
decades the expansion of HE has made taking a degree a norm
for middle-class young women. It is seen as a bridge between
adolescence and adulthood, a time of freedom, exploration
and finding romances. But what to do when one has finished?
Unless taking a vocational degree, our research suggests that
most middle-class women go to university like Drabble's
heroine lacking a vision of their future occupation. In this they
may differ from their male peers whose approach is more
planned and instrumental. After all, traditionally men have
been breadwinners, their identities defined by their job.

Two of the women whose stories are told here, Hannah
and Francesca (upper-middle-class), have found their way
into professional 'graduate-level' jobs. To succeed they drew
extensively on capitals from their family backgrounds, social,
cultural and economic, especially the latter. Without financial support from their parents, they would not have been
able to achieve these successes. Francesca's experiences in
seeking a legal career highlight the extensive barriers facing
working-class young people; the profession is ring-fenced in
favour of elite entrants. Similarly, the debt incurred in the
lengthy training to become a doctor is likely to deter all but
those with wealthy parents.

While those from the less prosperous ranks of the
middle-class share some of these advantages (knowhow,
parental advice, useful social contacts), the stories of Harriet
and Lauren show how those from more modest middle-class
backgrounds face more difficulties in the transition into the
labour market, as argued by Antonucci (2016). Both had to

work through their degrees to support themselves, unlike Hannah and Francesca. It was more difficult for them to build the kind of CVs recruiters look for, and their progress was slower. But both were able to retreat to the parental home as a way to facilitate job search. The knowledge that this option is always there provides a cushion for young middle-class women while they seek a vocation.

The conditions of the post-COVID precarious labour market present a tough environment for young people from lower-middle-class backgrounds as well as working-class graduates. The stories told here suggest that the fierce competition for professional jobs favours the reproduction and continuance of a wealthy upper-middle-class elite.

5

MAKING THEIR WAY: WORKING-CLASS MEN'S WORK STORIES

In terms of the broader youth employment market, young working-class men, especially those from white disadvantaged communities, are generally considered to be amongst the most 'at risk' and likely to be 'left behind' social groups, and are over-represented among those described as NEET (not in education, training or employment). However, our study shows that if working-class young men *do* make it to university and remain on the course (this group had the highest drop-out rate from university of our four categories), they can indeed achieve labour market success. They may take longer to do so however, due to lacking the levels of economic, social and cultural capital of their middle-class male peers, but they share with them the advantage of higher average earnings than those of women graduates. Our research shows that if they make it through university, they tend to be clearer about their next steps than the women covered in Chapter 4, particularly if they had chosen more vocational degree pathways.

Again we need to distinguish between the fractions or segments of the category 'working-class', since, as we will demonstrate, the upper-working-class male participants often hold an advantage over their 'firmly-working-class' peers, as is the case for young women in Chapter 6. This chapter considers the narratives of four young men. We categorized Shane and Kyle as 'firmly-working-class', whilst Justin and Rob were deemed 'upper-working-class' as explained in the following sections.

SHANE: A COMMITTED PUBLIC SERVANT?

Shane came from Brighton and was of mixed heritage – his mother is white British and his father is Sri Lankan. He had grown up with his mum, a single parent, and had no siblings. His mother was a secretary, whilst his father, with whom he had little contact, was an engineer who had moved to mainland Europe when Shane was much younger and remarried. Neither of his parents had been to university themselves, although some of his cousins had. Shane said of his class background 'I wouldn't consider us as middle-class', although he had 'grown up in a middle-class area' of the city.

As Shane came towards the end of his sixth form studies, he had decided not to go onto university, since he felt he had 'had enough of education', and 'didn't want to get up every day and go to classes'. He started working full-time in a local library after his A Levels, with a view to saving some money and travelling, which he managed to do for a 'gap year'. He remembered his reaction at school when the subject of applying to university was bought up:

> *When they started talking about it……it wasn't because I couldn't be arsed to do this Personal*

> *Statement but I was just like 'there's no point putting*
> *effort in if I'm not planning on going' because I*
> *didn't really want to do another 3 years of education.*
> *But then I started working and I was like 'I definitely*
> *don't want to start working full-time' as well,*
> *because I was just in a library doing like 9 'til 5 and it*
> *was horrid. So I was like 'the only thing to do is go to*
> *uni'. And then also all my mates that had started that*
> *year were like 'yeah it's amazing, you've got to go'…*
> *And I went to the UWE open day, that was the only*
> *open day I went to because I did mine like last*
> *minute, and I was like 'yeah, I could do this'.*

After Shane had made his mind up to apply to university, a year after he could have actually gone, his choice of institutions was largely informed by the issue of where he wanted to live, and apart from UWE, he decided not to attend any other open days:

> *I didn't really go to any open days because it was all*
> *like last minute, it was like a week before I was about*
> *to leave for Australia so I didn't have that much time,*
> *so I didn't have a chance to go to any open days*
> *apart from this one. And I was mostly just looking at*
> *like cities that I wanted to be in….and like the course*
> *obviously, and like any of the cities I thought I'd*
> *want to live in that run the course, rather than*
> *coming and looking at the uni.*

Shane chose to study Economics at UWE since it was the subject he had liked the most during his A Levels. He enjoyed his degree course and was already thinking of a career in economics, possibly as a researcher since the potential for travel in this line of work appealed to him. Shane was in receipt of a university bursary due to the low household income, and his mother also let out his bedroom whilst he was away and gave Shane the money she received for that. This modest additional income meant he didn't need to get part-time paid work whilst at university.

When we spoke with Shane at the start of his second year, his career plans had firmed up around the idea of working as a government economist, either as a civil servant or for some other government agencies. He was looking for placement opportunities to help him. He got a placement for his third year, taking the four year 'sandwich course' option, and worked in the finance department of a multinational office equipment firm, based in their UK headquarters on the outskirts of London.

Although he found the experience useful in terms of career planning, Shane didn't especially enjoy his placement year. He particularly missed having lie-ins and socializing with housemates since he was living in a shared house with people he didn't know too well. It made him realize 'how chilled uni was', previously thinking 'having two deadlines every year was like hard work, but it's just not!' The experience made him appreciate his remaining time at university more, and he was looking forward to his final year, although the majority of his friends from university had graduated by the time he returned to Bristol, and some had already left the city. He also missed the excitement of 'living in a uni town' whilst on his placement. He certainly felt there were some benefits though:

> *I think overall a really good experience, I kind of do miss uni though, uni life. But I just think that, yeah, the benefit of like having a placement here for when I graduate is really good motivation for me to carry on working, and also it's like my first real glimpse of like 9 to 5 work. So yeah overall it's a good experience.*

The placement year had offered Shane an insight into working in a graduate role, and he had considered switching his career focus from economics to accountancy. However, when we next spoke to Shane in late 2014, he had graduated from university with a first-class degree, and had started working as a government economist, having joined through the civil service graduate recruitment scheme. He had moved to London and was living as a lodger with one other person in an East End apartment. Shane said he had applied for 'about ten jobs' and 'stopped looking' when offered the civil service role. His placement year had proven invaluable in terms of offering experiences he could draw upon during the job application process, including at interview. Although he reflected that he had not really enjoyed the placement year, in hindsight it was 'definitely worth doing it', and he would recommend it to anyone.

Shane's civil service role meant he would be moving between government departments every few years, and gaining experience in a variety of increasingly senior roles. He had started on a salary of £32,500, and was enjoying annual increments and the possibility of a further pay rise through promotion in a few years' time. Shane expressed surprise at the relative lack of people in the civil service fast-stream scheme from 'newer' universities like UWE; it seemed as if almost everyone else was 'ex-public school' and had gone to a Russell Group institution. He enjoyed what he saw as the greater security offered in the public sector compared to some of his friends working in the more 'competitive' or even 'cut-throat' environment of the private sector. Shane also felt that there was more trust placed in people at his career stage in the public sector too when comparing experiences with some of his peers from university who now worked for private companies:

> *Compared to some of my friends that are in grad*
> *schemes I've been given like more responsibility off*
> *the bat and, yeah, just feels like a better experience so*
> *far.*

Shane also felt the public sector was more likely to support career development through further study, which was something he could benefit from directly as he was considering doing a Master's degree in Economics:

> *So that's another thing that I'm conscious of...*
> *another factor that is pushing my decision towards*
> *staying here...I'd probably do it before I finish*
> *because I know if you've got a Master's you've*
> *probably got a better chance of getting to Grade 7. I*
> *think it's becoming more of a like unwritten*
> *requirement in a way. So it's something that I'll*
> *probably be considering over the next year maybe,*
> *applying for it the year after or something.*

Since working as a civil servant Shane had also found his political views changing, moving 'towards the left', and he had become much more environmentally conscious than he'd been as a student. His civil service role had led to him working with economists from overseas too, re-igniting the earlier ambitions he'd expressed when we first met him as an undergraduate to travel and work abroad.

When we last met Shane in 2017, he had moved to the Treasury itself and was working on post-Brexit economic planning, something he was enjoying despite having been a keen 'remainer' who had strongly opposed Brexit personally. He was still living as a lodger in East London, but was considering moving to another part of the city to live with old friends from Brighton who had also relocated to London after finishing university. When asked to reflect on the extent to which his mixed ethnic Anglo/Asian heritage had impacted on his experiences of both university and work following graduation, he felt that it hadn't especially, although he did have a friend at the Treasury with West Indian heritage and they apparently joked about being the 'diversity quotient' in their team.

In autumn 2021, Shane reported that he was still living in London, renting with friends. He had left the civil service but was working as an economist in a public regulatory body, and earning £50–60,000. Shane was an excellent example of someone who had achieved social mobility and a highly successful transition out of university.

KYLE: 'I'M NOT THE TYPICAL STUDENT'

Kyle grew up close to Bristol in the smaller neighbouring city of Bath. His parents had separated when he was eight, and he grew up largely with his mother, who was a special needs support worker in a nearby college. He had one sibling – an older brother who was in his final year of university when we first met Kyle in 2010. He saw his father, who was a lorry driver and lived in another town in the region, every few months or so. Neither parent had gone to university themselves.

Kyle had long held ambitions to become a lawyer, specifically a barrister, which he partially attributed to having grown up in relatively poor circumstances:

(Neither)…my Mum or Dad have gone to university and through my life I've sort of seen the impacts of that…like throughout my whole life my Mum's never had any money, and neither has my Dad really…my whole life has just seen them struggling through debts

*and I just thought 'well I can't be bothered to handle
that', I've seen that growing up young and it's been a
stress in my life as well really. Because although
when I'm a child they might think 'oh he doesn't
worry about things like that, we're the adults who
worry about that', even as a child your perceptions
about what's going on financially in your house does
worry you because you know it has repercussions on
you. So I've always thought like I don't want to be in
that position, I'm going to work like hard and get a
job hopefully that will earn me loads of money,
which is why I want to be a barrister.*

Kyle had hoped to go to the University of Bristol to study
Law, but just missed out on the AAA grade A Level target of
his offer. He achieved AAB instead, so choosing to stay close
to his family, friends and his long-term girlfriend, Kyle
attended UWE, his 'insurance offer'. His other university
applications had also all been to reasonably nearby cities. Kyle
felt the change of employment opportunities for his generation
keenly, and feared the consequences of trying to find well-paid
work without a degree:

*I always just thought it would be a waste if I didn't
go to university....I think also I felt pressurized, but
more by society to go and get a degree, because I
think nowadays if you go to a job interview for a job
which is quite well paid they're going to expect you
to have a degree now...my generation is just going to
be the "degree generation" everyone's going to have
a degree, so it's just how you can distinguish yourself
from those other people, and if that's the base rate
you've got to at least get yourself a degree. So...
obviously if I want to be a lawyer it's definitely got to
be done.*

Kyle could trace his interest in law back a long time. He said he'd always been interested in how society was structured and how it works, and saw law as underpinning all of that. He was interested in the moral foundations of law and law-making, also acknowledging the potentially massive impact of law upon individual lives, either to redress wrongs or in punishing the lawbreakers. His career plan at the first interview was to complete his Law degree, then train further as a barrister through the Bristol Law School, a collaborative venture between the two Bristol universities, and based at UWE. Kyle's original intention was to live at home with his mum and commute to university daily, but he realized it would only cost slightly more to live in central Bristol, which would save him significant time on the daily commute. Kyle found a student flat which he shared with his girlfriend, who was also studying in the city. He had a part-time job in a clothes shop in Bath where he continued to work throughout his undergraduate years, travelling back from Bristol to work at weekends.

By the end of his first year, Kyle had had a change of plan regarding his intended career, moving away from the idea of practising law as a barrister or even a solicitor, and moving into law enforcement:

> *Now I kind of feel that I want to get into the police force, like special organized crime agency, or even like crime scene investigation. And I know like with a Law degree you can move up faster, and you can move into the police force at like a higher level...I've kind of completely done a U-turn on what I was going to do....I mean most of it was based on the fact that we did some modules in our first year that was about learning about being a barrister and stuff, and you just realize that your job as a barrister is such....you're basically going to be manipulating the*

> *law....for your financial gain, even if you know*
> *someone's guilty for example, and I think my*
> *approach to law is more of like moral, like actually*
> *applying the law.*

Kyle also felt that given his own working-class back-ground, he would be more suited to policing than to being a barrister, given his social skills and ability to work with people from 'regular' backgrounds rather than only moving in the upper echelons of society as he thought barristers would. He remained convinced that he was intellectually capable of being a barrister, but no longer felt as driven to achieve it, acknowledging he would be unable to do so without the necessary drive and absolute dedication demanded. His intended choice of career had surprised a number of people who had known Kyle well, including many of his friends and his mother:

> *My Mum's always said that I have a problem with*
> *authority, but I guess my problem is not the*
> *authority itself, it's just the way that a lot of those*
> *people handle their authority and use their authority*
> *which really pisses me off. Like if you've got*
> *authority that should be something that you should*
> *be proud of, use it effectively to help the community*
> *and help people, and not use it and seem to get on*
> *some massive power trip off it.*

Kyle remained committed to the idea of working for the police in a specialist forensic role or working in a serious crime unit throughout his second year. He felt encouraged by the manner in which the police were then restructuring their training, since he would be advantaged in terms of career progression as a graduate, and was confident his legal knowledge would further help him in that role. He had experienced some personal difficulties during his second year, and failed one of his modules meaning he would not be able to train as either a barrister or solicitor without re-doing and passing it. By the start of his third year, Kyle had moved back to Bath and was living with his girlfriend and some other friends. He seemed to have accommodated the fact that he would not become a practising lawyer into his future plans:

> I mean I always kind of thought that I'd be able to get a First, I think I have the sort of base level intelligence to do so. But....stuff that has happened, and plus I've sort of sometimes lacked in motivation because I've sort of fallen afield of what I initially wanted to do, which was to be a Barrister, so some of the modules I haven't engaged with because I sort of lacked in enthusiasm towards some of the subjects. But generally I think if I come out of it with a 2:1 I'll be really happy. And I know sort of to go into the police force they're not looking for geniuses anyway, they're looking for people who have the knowledge and are going to be right for the job and have the enthusiasm for it, which I think with the modules I'm doing and the experience hopefully I'm going to get over a couple of years, I'll sort of have that.

He was however considering doing a Master's degree in Law to help with his future career prospects, and was able to undertake a placement during his third year working for the Crown Prosecution Service (CPS), which should also help. He remained wedded to the idea of joining the police after university (possibly after his Master's degree), and was considering volunteering as a special constable to get valuable policing experience and to offer a better insight into what the job would actually entail.

But by the end of his third year Kyle had reconsidered his career aspirations once again. He was now hoping to re-sit the module he failed the previous year, and then train as a barrister, after seeing another side to the role whilst on his placement at the CPS, and re-evaluating what he had previously considered to be the inevitably morally dubious aspect of the role:

> *Basically this year I've done six months one day a week work experience with the Crown Prosecution Service, which forms one of my modules, and I sort of learnt that....because before, what sort of put me off being a barrister was sort of the moral and the ethical problems behind it, but I've kind of realized that you don't have to go down that route, you can sort of work as an in-house prosecution advocate for the Crown Prosecution Service or you can just be a prosecution barrister. So I think that's the sort of route that I'll take, if I can.*

By now Kyle had moved out of the house he was sharing with his girlfriend and had moved in with his mother who had remarried and relocated to Bristol. He found this a less stressful alternative to living in Bath with the additional commuting it entailed. Kyle remained in a relationship with his girlfriend despite them no longer sharing a house. They were still considering moving in together again and having children in the longer term. Kyle reflected back on his changing career aspirations, noting that he was effectively back where he had started when we first met him nearly three years earlier:

> *Yeah I've kind of gone from starting off wanting to be a barrister, then thought 'I'll take the easy route of being a solicitor', then 'I wouldn't mind being a*

> *forensic analyst for the police' then 'hey why don't I*
> *just become a policeman', and now I want to be a*
> *barrister again. Yeah, so been on a bit of a journey,*
> *yeah. I think mostly because I just didn't know what*
> *I wanted to do and I was kind of grasping at stuff*
> *which I thought I would enjoy, like the whole*
> *forensic thing, I really enjoyed the forensic science*
> *module I did, but then realising I don't actually know*
> *that much about science, so I'll probably have to go*
> *and do two or three Master's courses in chemistry*
> *and stuff...But I do think the barrister route would*
> *be the sort of a way for me, hopefully.*

He even talked of a longer-term plan of becoming a Queen's Counsel, and then a judge. Kyle had rated his overall university undergraduate experience at 8.5.

We next spoke with Kyle nearly 18 months later, in the second half of 2014, just over a year after he had graduated. He was working in a residential support unit for adults with learning difficulties, something he really enjoyed, and saving up money for his Law Master's course, which he decided to do at UoB rather than UWE. Kyle also volunteered with the Youth Offender Team in Bristol, supporting vulnerable young people in custody. His biggest news though was outside his working life; his girlfriend was pregnant with twins! Her family had bought a house for them in Bath, although Kyle was still living with his mother and her new husband in Bristol since it was less stressful for him, particularly whilst he was still studying.

Across the next two years, Kyle studied part-time for his Master's in law, for which he received a distinction, while working part-time in the care home. He lived between the house of his girlfriend and children in Bath, and of his mother and husband in Bristol. He explained the appeal of this arrangement:

> *I think it's good for me because, although the*
> *Master's is only part-time I put a lot of hours into it*
> *and it does take up a lot of my time, and then*
> *obviously working as well. So it would be really*
> *difficult if I were to have to do all of that and then*
> *every day come home and expect to do the full-on*
> *father thing and then wake up in the middle of the*
> *night and just be knackered the whole time. I think I*
> *would just be too tired to do it.*

He had also spent the intervening period re-sitting the module he had failed in his second year, and had passed it, meaning he could choose to pursue a career as a barrister or solicitor if he undertook the requisite additional study.

The final time we met Kyle in 2017, he was employed as a paralegal for a Bristol solicitors' firm. His career aspirations had moved on again, and he wasn't certain just what he wanted to do. His experience of working for a solicitor had not been as enjoyable as anticipated, largely since he spent 'too long sitting in an office and working on a computer':

> *I mean since having the twins I've kind of realized the*
> *importance of doing something which allows me to*
> *have some time, and if I was going to become a*
> *barrister I wouldn't have any time. I've also kind of*
> *realized the importance of doing something which*
> *actually you enjoy doing as opposed to doing*
> *something for the money. I'm not really enjoying the*
> *position I'm in at the moment… if that is what being*
> *a solicitor is then I don't want to be a solicitor.*

Kyle had rather lost his already faltering career drive the last time we saw him. The idea of working in criminal law still appealed, but he wasn't confident it was what he really wanted. When asked to think about his future career aspirations, and whose working lives he would like to emulate, he suggested:

> *I think originally it would have been people who were very successful within the legal field earning a lot of money. And then actually you kind of realize, even when you work for these big law firms where there are people earning lots of money, if you speak to them they still say, on Thursday they will say 'oh it's almost Friday, it's almost the weekend, thank God today is over'. And it's just like 'you don't enjoy it, you're getting paid hundreds of thousands of pounds a year but ultimately you're still working for two days at the end of a week!'. So I think actually I kind of lost being inspired to those type of people who are going to look back when they're sort of 65/ 70 and be like 'well what did I do, I didn't enjoy any of that, I got loads of money from it but...' So I don't really have any sort of idols or get inspiration from anyone really.*

In autumn 2021, Kyle was still working as a paralegal in a Bristol firm, albeit a criminal law paralegal, something closer to what his aspirations had been last time we had discussed them. Like Dylan in Chapter 3 and Francesca in Chapter 4, his aspirations of a career as a barrister had cooled, in part due to his acknowledging the reality of how difficult it is to achieve, especially for Kyle who lacked the valuable middle-class capitals upon which both Dylan and Francesca could draw.

JUSTIN: 'JUST A FISH IN A POND'

Justin, who had one sibling (a younger brother), comes from the Greater London area and has an upper-working-class background. His father is a self-employed window cleaner and taxi driver, whilst his mother is a secretary; neither of them attended university. His parents were always supportive and encouraging of Justin's education, and were integral to sending him to a church school some distance from home rather than the local comprehensive school, since they felt it offered a better chance of giving Justin access to a 'good' education. They were also keen for him to attend an 'old' university such as Bristol rather than a newer one like UWE. Justin did well in his A Levels – he got three grade As and chose to study Psychology at UoB. He remembers being clear when younger about his own educational ambitions:

> As a child I…distinctly remember thinking 'GCSEs,
> A levels, university' rather than 'GCSEs, diploma or
> BTEC' or anything like that, no apprenticeship or
> anything like that…I was always inclined that
> university is the one after A levels….I don't think I'd
> have done much else to be fair, I was never attracted
> by the idea of an apprenticeship or anything like that.
> But I would imagine that that would have been quite
> significant from an early age, thinking that university
> was the logical next step.

Like many of the young people featured in this book, Justin had no clear career aspiration when he started university, or throughout his first year. He had vaguely considered both advertizing and forensic psychology, but was not especially committed to either. He had found the transition to university study quite challenging, not in terms of the difficulty of the work itself, but more in terms of the inevitable comparisons he made with his peers:

> *Back in A level and GCSE I was always....I sound so arrogant, but I was always out-performing everyone else. But here it's like mid-way kind of....so I think I've got ridiculously high standards for myself, and coming to university it's kind of questioned those a little...It's weird from going from being 'a big fish in a little pond' to just being 'a fish in a pond'.*

Justin had worked part-time before university at a day care centre for children with special needs, and continued that work during his longer holidays from university. During his second year, he realized this could be a potential career route to pursue:

> *I'm thinking for the last three years I've had a job working with kids with developmental disorders, I've done volunteering work with adults with developmental disorders, I'm studying Psychology and the bit that I like the most is the bit about developmental disorders. I think there's a path emerging!*

At the start of Justin's third year, he told us that he had a stronger idea of his career plans than previously. He had continued working at the centre for children with special educational needs over his summer break:

> *I think over the summer I had a bit of an epiphany about that, so I figure now I'm going to take a year out, work in a school and then go on to an Educational Psychology programme...I've been looking at (Educational Psychology) programmes here, they've got a Master's and a couple of*

> *doctorates here in Bath and Cardiff and that way, so*
> *I'm thinking about that.*

Justin had started volunteering at a social night for adults with Asperger's syndrome in a Bristol pub when he returned from his summer break, to give him further valuable experience. By the end of his final year, he had also started volunteering at a primary school in Bristol, as a support worker for a reception class, giving him more practical experience and offering an opportunity to experience a school setting. He was still aiming longer term towards an educational psychologist qualification, but that required several years' teaching experience first. He intended applying for a PGCE primary school teaching qualification at UWE, since UoB did not offer such an award. Justin had a new girlfriend from university, and she was also planning to do the UWE primary PGCE, further incentivizing him to stay in the city rather than go elsewhere for his teaching qualification – this 'was definitely having an impact' on his choices and plans.

Justin had a five-year plan by the end of his undergraduate course; to qualify as a teacher, get some experience in schools, then do an educational psychologist qualification and move into that field. He felt he was finishing university as a much rounder, more experienced and more socially aware person than when he'd arrived at university:

> *I think when I started I was quite happy in my own*
> *little world doing my own little thing, because I'd*
> *never really been out of London I thought I was*
> *quite happy how it is. And now I've seen different*
> *parts of the country and been to different places in*
> *the world, I want to do more of that and I want to*
> *see more.*

It was nearly two years until we spoke to Justin again, by when he had graduated with a first-class degree, spent a year working as a teaching assistant in a multi-cultural inner-city secondary school in Bristol, and started the PGCE in primary teaching at UWE. He was still with his girlfriend, who had completed her PGCE whilst Justin was working as a teaching assistant, and now had a job as a primary school teacher in Bristol. They were planning a future together, including buying a house, getting married and having children. Justin spoke of teaching being 'plan B' if becoming an educational psychologist didn't work out; he would be perfectly happy with that. Justin now considered Bristol as home, a process accelerated by his parents breaking up and divorcing since we last spoke to him, meaning he felt less of a connection to his family home and his pre-student life.

When we last met Justin in April 2017, he reflected happily on his life since the project started in 2010. He was working as a teacher in Bristol and had bought a house with his girlfriend, to whom he was by then engaged, with the wedding set for about a year hence. As much as he enjoyed his career, he valued other things as more important, and reflected on his time at university very positively, suggesting he'd learnt a lot of valuable skills:

> *I learnt all of that when I was at uni, cooking for myself, all of that. I think maturity has come from that as well, I've never gone back home, I've never gone back to live with my parents or taken anything from anyone else. Like my Dad sends me a bit of money every month but it's not enough to... -you know I went to uni, I met my girlfriend there, we bought a house, we're getting married, both got jobs. If I'd not gone to uni I don't think I'd have that. And to me, my career is less important than all of those*

things. I've got a house – how many other people my
age have bought a house?

His teaching experiences had caused Justin to re-evaluate what he considered the purpose of education was in contemporary society, feeling the emphasis in schools was wrong:

I think there's too much focus on making sure that
children can use subordinate clauses and write in the
past progressive tense, whereas actually if they are a
decent person and able to function...if they know
how to learn, once they leave school they're probably
better than whether they can write in the past tense

Interestingly Justin felt his parents were disappointed in his career choice, feeling he could have achieved something more prestigious given his A level grades and first-class degree from UoB. Perhaps this was due to their own classed aspirations, and how they had seen Justin as carrying those for the family.

In autumn 2021, Justin reported that he was now married and living in Birmingham where his wife's family lived. He was working as a primary school teacher, owned his own house and was earning £30–40,000. He was very satisfied with his life and, like many of the other young people we feature in this book, not driven by the need to maximize his income.

ROB: SEEKING SAFETY AND SECURITY

Rob grew up in a small rural town about an hour's drive away from Bristol, where he lived with his mother, a nursing auxiliary, and his father, a self-employed agricultural engineer. For as long as he could remember, Rob had always intended being an engineer too, and he chose his A Levels accordingly. Rob, an only child, had attended an independent school as a non-boarding 'day pupil'. Rob's parents had inherited some money which they used to pay for his education, apparently having believed he had been 'held back' at his state school previously. Despite having attended a fee-paying school, his family income was such that Rob, like Justin, was given a small bursary from the university, and he also qualified for a larger one from a local charity. Rob had been attracted to UWE to study Engineering in part because of its proximity to his home town (he commuted daily to university rather than live in Bristol) and partly because of its strong reputation in the field, for instance, with the 'Bloodhound' world land-speed record vehicle.

Although Rob had attended a private school, he had not felt much affinity with many of his fellow pupils, most of whom were from financially better-off backgrounds, and, for Rob, failed to appreciate how fortunate they were:

> *People just had this sense of automatic entitlement...*
> *Most people weren't too bad but you got some who*
> *just had it too easy in life because their parents just*
> *had almost more money than sense...they've been*
> *given a great opportunity by going to a school like*
> *that to get the best opportunity in life...While a*
> *private school's good for typically getting grades and*
> *things like that, it's not great at teaching life lessons,*
> *because obviously they've just grown up with so*
> *much money and they just felt that everything just*
> *falls into their lap.*

Rob felt he would not have been able to achieve his career goal of becoming 'a mechanical design engineer' without attending university, especially given the relatively poor employment situation in his home town; there were very few opportunities for an appropriate apprenticeship. He was interested in design, 'because I enjoy the design aspect of engineering, sort of looking at the problem first and then working through the steps to find the best solution to that problem'. Rob's course offered two options by way of routes, a three-year BSc, or a four-year MSc, for those who achieved sufficiently high grades in their first two years. Rob was keen to take the higher-level award from the outset, since he felt a Master's level qualification would offer enhanced opportunities for career progression. In what he considered the unlikely event of not enjoying working as an engineer, Rob was aware that the qualification could be used to access other careers as well, meaning he could 'then look at doing something else'.

Rob worked hard on his course, for an estimated 40 or 50 hours a week, more than the vast majority of those in the study:

> ...even on a Saturday morning or Sunday morning I'll still do maybe an hour to 3 hours, and then do something for the rest of the day and then maybe still an hour before I go to bed...It would be nice if I could get away with doing less, but I want to get a decent grade.

His personal motivation to succeed was impressive. He spent a long time applying for internships in engineering firms too, but was desperate to achieve things through his own efforts rather than those of someone else such as a family member. Indeed, he was fairly scathing, contemptuous even, of people he knew who were doing that (see Abrahams, 2017):

> Because I wouldn't want my family to help me because I want to be able to say 'I've achieved this without the help of someone else', whereas some of my friends from school are very much relying on who their grandparents or parents know to get them a job

at the end of it, which I don't agree with because if
your parents have managed to get a career for
themselves, why can't you?

By the time we next spoke with Rob in early 2015, he was working as a graduate recruit at the Bristol site of an international engineering company. He had completed his Master's qualification, achieving a merit grade. He had been relatively successful in his attempts to find work – he was invited to 'about ten interviews' but attended only two of them and was offered both jobs. He was enjoying his job; it was a well-structured training system for graduate recruits and involved a fixed period on placements in a range of departments to provide a broad experience of the company's work:

I'm happy where I am for now. They're putting me
through certain professional development schemes...
well it wouldn't make sense to leave those schemes,
so stay then until those are completed and then I'm
more employable once I've got those accreditations
against my name, make me more employable. I can
then look potentially to go elsewhere and get another
job. But at the moment I'm happy where I am and
the projects are interesting.

Prior to starting that role, Rob had taken a strategic approach to securing employment:

I wanted to get my foot in the door somewhere,
because once you've got your foot in the door it was
going to be much easier to then move on. Whereas if
you haven't...put yourself into that initial position,
you can't then go on to further yourself...I'd done a
placement (previously) which I organized myself. I
got in for my last exam in my third year and went 'I

*need experience' and just phoned every company in
my area until somebody said yes. And I ended up
with two offers. So persistence works.*

By the time we last saw Rob, he felt his life had settled
nicely. He was still working for the same company he had
joined from university, and had bought a house with his
girlfriend to whom he was now engaged. The house was near
the town where they both grew up. He spoke of future plans
for children, but in the meantime they had bought a dog.

In autumn 2021 Rob was still living in the same house and
working for the same company. He was now married and was
earning £40–50,000. He reported being very happy with his
life.

CONCLUSION

Although they have some things in common – high academic
achievement for instance – the narrative accounts of the four
young working-class men reveal the highly individualized
nature of the journey into, through and out of university and
into the graduate careers market. These were in part informed
by personal circumstances or family events – Kyle's girlfriend
becoming pregnant with twins, for instance, significantly
influenced his options, and partly by their own classed backgrounds, which is the focus of our study. As explained in
Chapter 2, we used a multi-factorial approach to categorizing
the project's participants in terms of their social class. For
some participants, the appropriate category was readily
apparent as we explain there, but for others, it was less clearly
so. This class demarcation is further complicated when we
drill into one particular grouping in order to better understand
the background and experiences of the different fractions of a

given class. We categorized Shane and Kyle as 'firmly-working-class', and Justin and Rob as 'upper-working-class'. This was not simply due to parental occupations but an acknowledgement of other influences upon the lives of the young men in question.

Justin attended a selective church school, and Rob, an independent fee-paying school – whilst Shane and Kyle had gone to their local state 'comprehensive' schools. For both Rob and Justin, their whole school set-up was geared towards achieving educational success and progression into university, and most of their peers from school did indeed follow that route. There was a family expectation on Rob and Justin that they would go to university, but this was not true of either Kyle or Shane.

Another source of relative advantage and enhanced educational opportunities for Justin and Rob was that they grew up in homes with two incomes. This is something that would significantly influence their experiences as there would have been more disposable income available in the households, compared to the childhood experiences of Kyle and Shane who both lived with their mother as the only 'breadwinner'; and both mothers were in relatively low-paid employment. Kyle needed to work part-time in a shop whilst an undergraduate student. Shane escaped this because of his mum letting out his bedroom and giving him the rent. Neither Justin nor Rob took paid work during university term, meaning they had more time to study or join in with social activities and enjoy the fuller 'student experience', from which those highlighted in the two chapters on middle-class participants benefitted (e.g. Francesca in Chapter 4).

6

CONFRONTING DOUBLE DISADVANTAGE: WORKING-CLASS WOMEN

This chapter explores the narratives of the working-class women graduates. It could be presumed that once working-class women graduate from university, their opportunities to access secure employment mirror those of their male peers from more affluent backgrounds. If higher education was truly a great leveller, then surely this would be a reality. However, what our research uncovered and this chapter will demonstrate is that gender and class disadvantage combine to put working-class women in a doubly disadvantaged position.

Further, we know that, like the three groups in the preceding chapters, 'working-class women' are not a homogenous group, far from it. There are divisions within the group based on demographic characteristics and the resources (capitals) available to these women. There are 'firmly-' and 'upper-' working-class groups within the 'working-class' category. Those who have cultural, social and economic capital which is considered 'working-class' we judged to be 'firmly- working-class'. Those who have the cultural and social capital typically considered 'working-class' but the economic capital typically found among the lower-middle-classes, or a similar configuration, are what we refer to as 'upper-working-class'. These women are often 'better' positioned than those from firmly-working-class backgrounds to draw on resources in the graduate labour market to find 'professional' employment. The trajectories of three-firmly working-class women and one upper-working-class woman are explored in this chapter.

When the young working-class women in this study accessed university in 2010, most did so with 'high' aspirations. They saw university as a route through which they could enter professions such as journalism, law, finance, engineering, politics, and the civil service. However, like the middle-class women in Chapter 4, they experienced a 'cooling' or 'dampening-down' of their initial aspirations as they struggled to imagine how they could have both a successful career and be a mother. Due to this, they turned away from these male-dominated professions to ones considered to be more conducive with motherhood. For example, two of the women in the study arrived at university with aspirations to go into teaching, but by graduation 11 were either considering or working towards becoming a teacher. One major contributing reason for this was the perceived compatibility of being a teacher and raising a family.

It is important to note that the working-class women also moved away from careers dominated by the middle-classes and towards jobs which they felt 'people like them' did. For example, Sophie arrived at university with aspirations to work in the civil service in London: after graduation she began searching for apprenticeships at her local council. Others arrived with aspirations to do research, to get into writing and publishing, and become museum curators. Upon graduation they had been steered away from these professions, which are dominated by the middle-classes, and most were considering entering teaching. This is not uncommon: historically, teaching has been considered a 'respectable' occupation for working-class women which offers a promise of upward social mobility (Morrison, 2014).

Further, they viewed entering teaching and other female-dominated professions, such as care work and social work, as routes through which they could achieve an additional aspiration: to make a positive contribution to their communities, to 'make a difference'. However, in some cases this left them navigating exploitation in the workplace because, as noted in Chapter 4, occupations that are dominated by women are less well paid and considered less socially valuable.

In this chapter, we explore the ways in which gender, class position and the status of the university attended by the women impacted on their transitions out of university and their trajectories in the labour market. First, we examine the story of Melissa, a graduate of English who achieved a first-class honours degree. Melissa is a white British young woman from an upper working-class background. Her father left education after completing his O Levels to become a factory worker and her stepmother attended nursing college to train to work as a nurse. Upon arriving at university, Melissa had 'working-class' cultural and social capital but had the support of her family's lower-middle-class economic capital. Then we will meet Adele, a Black young woman from Wales who achieved an upper second-class (2:1) degree in History and International Relations from UWE. Adele is from a firmly working-class background, that is, her cultural, social and economic capital was synonymous with being 'working-class'.

Next is Jackie, a white British graduate of Sociology who achieved an upper second-class degree from the University of Bristol. Like Adele, Jackie was from a firmly-working-class background from London. As was Sariah, whom we meet next. Sariah, a Black British graduate of UWE, studied sociology and achieved an upper second-class degree.

All four young women attempted to draw on the capital they have within their remit to find secure, professional employment after graduation. However, the opportunities available to them are due, in part, to their backgrounds (whether they are firmly-, or upper-, working-class) and the cachet associated with the university through which they obtained their degree.

MELISSA'S STORY: 'JUST A COMMON STATE SCHOOL GIRL'

Melissa is a white upper-working-class woman from a small town in Sussex. There she and her two siblings were raised by her father, who passed away before she arrived at university, and her stepmother. Like all the working-class women discussed in this chapter, Melissa attended a state school and her local college. She had been encouraged by her teachers to submit an application to Cambridge. Reflecting on her interview at the university she said:

> *When I was there I didn't feel like I really kind of clicked with the university, so I think I'm glad that I had an interview and had a chance to see that I didn't think it was really for me. [...] I constantly felt like I was inflecting that I'm a state school person. And I really don't like that about myself, just getting really intimidated by people like that and feeling 'oh I'm just a common state school girl, I don't know anything'.*

When she arrived at UoB to study English, Melissa articulated her position as 'in-between' class-based spaces and groups; she did not feel a sense of 'fit' in spheres dominated by the working-classes, nor those dominated by the middle-classes. One marker of this, she noted, was her accent and how it was perceived by different groups:

> At home I'm normally like regarded as like, I don't know…a bit more well-spoken, but coming here [to UoB] everyone sounds quite middle-class.

Although she experienced some social anxiety upon arriving at university, Melissa soon made friends with other students on her undergraduate course. She managed to assimilate with some of the students whom she lived alongside in halls of residence. However, she noted cultural 'differences' between herself and those who had previously attended private schools and reported she 'did not necessarily fit in in that way'.

While the remaining women in this chapter arrived at university in pursuit of careers within specific employment sectors, Melissa demonstrated no sense of urgency to begin crafting her career goals. Her approach was similar to those demonstrated by the middle-class women in Chapter 4, and some of the men in Chapters 3 and 5. When asked about her career aspirations, she said:

> I suppose because I don't really know at all what I want to do after university, I'm hoping like kind of during the course of this I'll find something that I want to specialize in, either like career-wise or taking like a post-grad course or something. […] I don't know what I want to do with my life, so I'm kind of hoping that in the next 3 years I'll work that bit out.

Unlike the rest of the women in this chapter, Melissa did not need to engage in paid work out of necessity during undergraduate studies. However, she worked during the summer breaks as a waitress in order to fund her travels around Europe and Africa. As she did not need to engage in term-time employment in order to pay for necessities, she had the capacity to participate in extracurricular activities. Throughout her undergraduate degree she wrote for the university newspaper, became President of the English Society and played the violin in the university's orchestra.

Melissa wanted to do an internship during the summer holidays alongside working as a waitress because she believed the latter 'doesn't really count' as valuable work experience to most graduate employers. Her aim when applying for internships was to explore the potential employment opportunities available to her after graduation. When searching for internships in publishing and journalism, she found that all the opportunities were unpaid. However, this was not an issue for Melissa as she had economic capital in her savings account and from family inheritance. As this was the case, she was able to support herself whilst engaged in unpaid work for two graduate employers.

Both internships were full-time, spanned a six-week period and were in publishing and journalism. One was with a 'top 10' graduate recruiter, the other with an independent publisher of academic work. She discovered the internships through attending an open day where employers came to the UoB to discuss career opportunities with students:

> *The editor came and did a talk at the postgrad open day and I just kind of emailed her afterwards like asking her if she had any advice because she was talking about work experience and I kind of told her I'd done some student media stuff and she emailed me back telling me to send my CV. So that was quite*

*easy. They had like a little interview but it was quite
informal.*

Russell Group universities are known targets of most
elite graduate employers. In 2017, UoB was the fourth most
targeted university by the 'top' graduate recruiters (e.g. the
BBC, Goldman Sachs, HSBC, PwC and TeachFirst). On the
list of the 25 most targeted universities in the UK, all were
Russell Group and/or 'ancient' universities (High fliers, 2018).
The perceived prestigious cachet of these universities influences
graduate employers' perceptions of the graduates from these
institutions as being 'among the best'. This cachet is also one
that drives students to apply to these institutions as they are
well-known entry points to professional employment. However,
this was not a motivating factor for Melissa applying to
UoB, as when talking about her future orientations towards
employment she said:

> *I'm not a very career-orientated person as you might
> have guessed. I try not to think too far in the future,
> I'm not that bothered about kind of making money
> from my career. I've done the internships because I
> enjoy them and then if they're going to help my
> career that's kind of a perk. Like I've never been one
> of those people who does things just to put stuff on
> their CV.*

As noted in preceding chapters, internships and extracurricular facilitate access to many high-status, high-salaried
employment opportunities, and lead graduates to feel more
positive about their future career prospects compared to those
unable to take part in such activities. However, access to these
opportunities usually requires high-value social, cultural and
economic capital, most often passed on by family members
and caregivers.

As Melissa neared the end of her degree she applied to study a Master's in European literature at UoB. Her rationale behind this was simple: to postpone the career decision-making process:

> *If I wasn't doing a Master's and going straight into work I wouldn't feel ready but that's basically the reason that I'm doing a Master's. I don't really know what I want to do as a career, so I want to delay that for a bit longer.*

Melissa achieved a first-class honours degree and then graduated from her Master's in 2014. She was not actively searching for employment when she came across the opportunity to do another full-time internship, this time at a 'top ten' UK social network site. The job was located in London, offered a six-month contract and paid £250 per week. Unlike the remaining working-class women in this chapter, Melissa shared no concern over the precarious employment contract, the salary which paid £7 per hour and demonstrated no sense of immediacy to earn a higher wage.

Through the social capital she had accumulated at university, she was able to stay at a friend's family home. Before moving to London she had only met her friend's parents once before they invited her to move in, free of charge:

> *I was going to like stay with different friends for a few weeks each just to kind of save a bit of money and not have to pay rent straightaway, and then they [friend's parents] kind of haven't said anything about me leaving, so I'm just staying there for as long as I can because I'm not paying any rent.*

Like many other young graduates, Melissa had planned to move to London and 'do different bits of work experience' regardless of whether she had secured the internship or not.

Engaging in numerous precarious contracts allows graduates to weave together their experiences to demonstrate that they have constructed a portfolio career. These are considered desirable by graduate employers. However, it tends only to be graduates from more affluent backgrounds who are able to participate, as engaging in precarious employment such as internships and volunteering requires a safety net of economic capital.

Mobilizing 'valuable' social capital is also key to accessing these opportunities. Melissa had little social capital within her family to draw on in order to find work:

> *My family wouldn't be the first... I'd probably go at it alone. I don't know how much, like even if they wanted to, how much they'd be able to help.*

However, the social capital she had amassed at university was plentiful. Perhaps this is one reason why Melissa defined herself as 'lower-middle-class' upon graduating. Most of the friends she had made during her time at university were from London originally, and those who were not had moved to London after university to begin working on graduate schemes. Utilizing this capital provided her with the access to work in London, a city which is referred to as the 'dominant winner region' and 'escalator region' (Hoare & Corver, 2010) as most of the growth in professional and managerial employment in recent decades has occurred there. Between 2012 and 2019, 45% of the growth in these roles nationwide has taken place in London (Social Mobility Commission, 2019).

Graduate jobs in London are highly sought after, and Melissa had to embark on a competitive process in order to secure the six-month internship. A total of 140 applicants had applied for the role; what supported her success in the interview was Melissa's demonstration of the skills she had acquired in the previous unpaid work experience she engaged in as a student.

Melissa was hopeful that she would be offered a permanent contract once the internship was over. Engaging in this internship had provided her with the opportunity to develop her career aspirations as she then aimed to find work as an editor. Though she wanted to continue working there, she understood that her prospects were not great as only one-third of the interns at that company are offered further work. Whether she was to remain at the company or not, she intended to stay in London as she wanted access to the employment opportunities that the city offered. The last time we met with Melissa she had a more refined idea of the employment trajectory that she wished to pursue, though it was not fixed:

> *I want to continue on the like editorial trajectory.*
> *Like I'm not kind of dead set on one job in particular*
> *but I think definitely doing something with words!*
> *Yeah, that kind of thing.*

Overall, university provided Melissa with the opportunity to acquire social and cultural capital that proved valuable upon graduation. This, as well as having the economic capital of a lower-middle-class woman, unlocked a trajectory which was close to that of the group of middle-class women in Chapter 4.

ADELE'S STORY: 'I NEED THAT JOB OTHERWISE I CAN'T REALLY SURVIVE'

Adele is a Black firmly-working-class woman from South Wales. She was raised alongside her older sister by her mother, a dinner lady and cleaner whom Adele described as 'just getting by day-to-day, trying to get money in'. Adele labelled herself an 'aspirational working-class' woman who wanted to follow in her sister's footsteps, to go to university and be upwardly socially mobile. Like the upwardly mobile working-class women in Lawler's (1999) work, Adele dreamt of 'escape' and embodied 'the fantasy of getting out and getting away'. She was thus part of the 'aspirational working class', a group which, to varying degrees, pursues the acquisition of resources and capital synonymous with a middle-class life.

Adele arrived at UWE to study History and International Relations aged 20, meaning she was two years older than the other women in this chapter when starting her degree. After completing her A Levels, Adele said that going to university 'just wasn't done, it's always in the back of my head "it's [university] not for you"'. The route which she felt expected to take at the age of 18 was:

> *Get a job, boring, manual 9 to 5 job and that was it, and you maybe have a relationship, you settle down and you earn.*

Following this, Adele spent two years either unemployed or in low-paid employment. She was forced to access benefits in order to survive, and this experience was one of the driving forces behind her applying to study at university:

> *At first I was like 'no, there's no way in hell I am going on benefits'. There's such a stigma around it. When I finally did sign on I just felt...I don't know, guilty and like the stigma attached to it. After I thought to myself 'I don't want to go back there' [...] 'I don't want to be like my Mum'. So, I was like 'Okay, I really want to go to uni'.*

Adele arrived at university with aspirations to enter journalism. She had already compiled a list of the businesses she aspired to work for, and she sought to secure internships with these companies as an undergraduate student. Like Jackie, and most of the other firmly working-class women, Adele outlined that while she was driven to earn 'money to survive', she wanted to engage in employment where she could make a difference, where her 'heart is in it'.

Twelve out of the 22 working-class women who took part in the first phase of the *Paired Peers* study had to take paid employment during term time in order to pay their bills. Almost all of these women were in precarious forms of employment, marked by low pay and unreliable hours. They worked as barmaids, cleaners and childminders, in retail or administration. This is a common phenomenon found in the narratives of undergraduate students from low socio-economic backgrounds. Due to these insecure conditions, many of the women experienced anxiety and were vulnerable to exploitation, including Adele:

> *I need that job otherwise I can't really survive, I can't really function.... It's so crucial to me being at uni, that part-time job, I'm constantly worrying 'am I doing OK in it? Does [MANAGER] like me?' because if she doesn't and she gets rid of me what am I going to do? Without work I literally don't know how I would cope. But still, you know, when I'm in the supermarket and, you know, you're buying 17p tins of beans. Everything is like Tesco Value, everything is like the cheapest you can get.*

It was not uncommon for Adele to work a twenty-hour week as a retail assistant, and due to this, she struggled to imagine how she would have the capacity to engage in an internship, which she acknowledged was crucial to her career development. An additional barrier to accessing an internship was the lack of economic capital to support herself while doing unpaid work, and a lack of social capital she had in the sector:

> *I'd love to go into journalism and I know that people are 'oh God that's so hard to get into, you need to know people in the right area'. I spoke to like my Sister about it and she was like 'if you want to go into it, do your best, like try and get an internship' which I'm looking into, trying to get an internship now somewhere. But I also work part-time, so it's trying to juggle doing my studies, working part-time and then doing an internship. I'd like to do one at the [NEWSPAPER], but they don't pay students.*

After graduating university with a 2:1, Adele began searching for relevant internships in Bristol, but she was unable to secure paid or unpaid work in journalism. Having little-to-no social capital in employment sectors dominated by the middle-classes is common for working-class students and graduates. Due to this, they are less likely than their more privileged counterparts to gain entry to access routes to formal and informal, unadvertized employment opportunities. As Adele continued to attempt to access paid internships, she saw how her more advantaged peers were better positioned to 'play the game' due to their capital composition and how this was favourably viewed by employers:

> *If you have somebody in your family that knows somebody else, so if your Dad's a businessman and you know that he has links with other people, it helps. I've seen it happen. Like in second year, my housemate was looking for a placement, her dad pulled a few strings and she got like a marketing position at a supermarket in London. We all knew there was no way in hell she would have got that if*

> *her Dad didn't have that contact, because you just*
> *wouldn't know those people. But because her Dad*
> *owns his own supermarket chain he knew them…*
> *It's all about who you know.*

Unlike the post-graduation narratives of the middle-class women, Adele's attempts to find work were marked by anxiety. She had limited time to secure paid employment that was relevant to her degree and aspirations, before she would have to return to a routine service occupation in order to survive:

> *I know for a fact if I don't find a job that I really*
> *want within… say by about September, I'm going to*
> *have to do a bar job, I'm going to have to do*
> *something so I can afford to pay my rent. Whereas*
> *some other people might be given a bit of time to*
> *maybe go travelling and to maybe think really what*
> *they want to do, what sort of action, and have a few*
> *trial and error kind of things, but I kind of can't, I*
> *haven't got that safety net, I haven't got the*
> *opportunity to muck up on too many occasions.*

This is a stark difference to Hannah's narrative in Chapter 4, which is marked by ample economic capital, and the cultural and social capital which enabled her to volunteer in different sectors before deciding on her next career move. Adele was not able to break into journalism after graduation, and so she took up work as a charity fundraiser officer starting on £18,500.

Though this is not traditionally considered a 'graduate job', Adele remarked that you had to have a degree in order to secure an interview. This experience was often shared by *Paired Peers* graduates: many found that job roles which would traditionally considered to be non-graduate are now 'crowded', as Elias and Purcell (2013) put it, by graduates.

Thus, employers are now expecting candidates to have degrees for roles which do not require the skills developed through a higher education experience.

This phenomenon has occurred because the 'stock' of graduate talent has sharply risen over the last 15 years, due in part to the efforts to expand HE, and the same growth has not been seen in the section of the labour market considered to require 'high-skilled graduates'. Adele reflected on the staff composition of her workplace, saying 'the younger ones have gone to uni, and the older ones haven't'. With Adele working in a 'non-traditional', or what Elias and Purcell (2013) would refer to as a 'new' graduate, job she found that her family struggled to understand her job:

> *If I was like a doctor then she'd get it and she'd be 'oh my Granddaughter's a doctor', but she doesn't like...get it. To her it's like it's not a traditionally... you know it's not a solid job to do...it's not traditionally like well-paid or anything.*

This was particularly difficult for Adele as, compared to the other working-class women in the study, she held pronounced aspirations for upward mobility. When articulating these she drew on the experiences of hardship she and her mother experienced. This was emblematic of Freie's (2010, p. 229) findings which demonstrated that working-class women discuss 'their future plans as stemming from, and informed by, life lessons they have learned from witnessing their mothers' struggles with family, employment and education'. While Adele was keen to secure a social distance from her mother, she also did not want to be considered middle-class. Instead, she wanted to be viewed as a particular type of working-class person. She remarked that her friends would regularly say:

'Oh you're middle-class', I'm like 'I'm not middle-class', I have this thing all the time. I say 'aspirational working-class'.

Unlike Melissa, who experienced a sense of unease about being in between class categories, Adele viewed this position as beneficial as it provided her with the tools to skilfully navigate her workspace. Adele said that she 'played' on her working-classness 'quite a bit as well sometimes in my job, which bodes quite well because I think people feel more comfortable'. She consciously engaged in this type of impression management when she was:

Around people who I know are like working-class or from that kind of background, I flip back to like my language and my behaviour being more kind of perhaps... and I feel like sometimes my Welsh accent comes out a bit more.

However, the great majority of her work colleagues were from more privileged backgrounds, and she described them as being from 'a completely different world' to her. When in conversation with these colleagues she held back her working-class cultural capital, particularly through her use of language and her accent:

If I'm in a meeting, and I'm in a meeting with quite senior people who are quite middle-class in their background and how they talk and how they have conversations, then I'll change and I'll make sure that my tone of voice and my language is more appropriate for that setting.

Adele's experiences were clearly marked by her class background and the hardship she and her mother had experienced. Overall, she had a good understanding of how to 'play the game', the rules of which her older sister had taught her and she observed her more privileged counterparts practising. However, coming from a firmly working-class background, she did not have the capitals to participate. Thus, she was not able to achieve her aspirations to enter journalism.

JACKIE'S STORY: 'I WANT TO CHANGE SOMETHING IN A POSITIVE WAY'

Jackie is a white firmly-working-class woman from South East London, where she was raised by her mother, a cleaner, and her father, an engineer. There she lived in a council house with her three younger siblings, two sisters and a brother, with whom she shared a bedroom. Due to her parents' low income, Jackie received the maximum student loan and grant from Student Finance England, as well as a university bursary, to study Sociology at UoB.

Jackie was the first person in her family 'to test university out'. Throughout her time at UoB Jackie showed strong family attachments, describing family as her 'everything, they're the centre of my universe'. This was particularly the case for her mother who she described as 'the most influential person' in her life who is 'central to everything' that she does:

> Wherever my Mum is usually I'm there as well, I like talking to her. We talk regularly on the phone, and like it's nice because now we have loads of things to tell each other every time we phone each other. Like we're on the phone for at least an hour a day.

The regular contact helped them maintain their close relationship throughout Jackie's time at university. Preserving this bond was key to Jackie's psychic survival as she became

upwardly socially mobile, as also found in the narratives of
upwardly mobile working-class women in Walkerdine and
Lucey's (1989) research. Both her parents and grandparents
had high aspirations for her; they had long hoped that she
would go to university and regularly expressed how proud
they were that she had done so. Jackie's mother, in particular,
had aspirations that her daughter would attend university in
order to find a job that she 'loves' and that also offers stability.
Throughout her studies, her mother reminded her often that
she could return home whenever she wanted to. When Jackie
faced challenges in Bristol, her mum would reach out to invite
her home:

> *Mum was like 'if you want to come home, you can*
> *come home'. And I was like 'Mum, I can't drop out'.*
> *And she was like 'just see, because if you really feel*
> *like it just remember you tried it, we'll support you,*
> *but if you want to come home there is always that*
> *option'.*

At times this offer was tempting to Jackie because, unlike
Melissa, she was not able to develop friendships with her
student peers at UoB that lasted beyond graduation. Like
many other working-class women in 'prestigious' higher
education institutions, Jackie felt like an outsider at the
Russell Group university, perceiving that many of her fellow
students 'didn't get' her and 'had no empathy' for
working-class people and their lived experiences. Second,
staff regularly used academic language which acted as a
barrier to her understanding the curriculum, and they made
assumptions about the cultural capital she held:

> *I don't always feel like I fit in seminars, just because*
> *of my background. Some seminar teachers, they*
> *make the assumption that everyone has come from a*

*privileged middle-class background. One day
[lecturer] was talking about children's experiences at
school, and he was saying that some children don't
have the cultural capital to access uni. And then he
said, 'oh but all of us at Bristol here must have been
taken to art galleries and gone on holidays to France
and skiing abroad' and I thought 'I've never been
abroad for a holiday in my life!'. I didn't say
anything because I don't ever say anything, but I was
just like…crazy assumptions.*

Jackie had two aspirations for her life after graduation: to return back to London to live once again in the family home and study for a PGCE. She began developing her aspiration to enter teaching at the age of 14 and had engaged in volunteer work in educational settings before arriving at university. She volunteered to be a teaching assistant in her sixth form college, had been a tutor to GCSE students and a reading-support assistant in a primary school. She participated in these roles with the aim of refining her aspirations, to explore which level she wanted to teach at, and she settled on primary. Jackie's goal had been fixed for some time, and she was highly driven:

*I really, really want to be a teacher. So I'm going to
go for it until I am one.*

Jackie's motivation to volunteer in an education setting was different from Melissa's, who had done some work in a school in Asia prior to her undergraduate studies to fulfil her aspirations to travel. The latter has grown to be a popular option for young people, and through embarking on these experiences, they are able to demonstrate good 'global citizenship' and develop a form of cultural capital which is valued by graduate employers.

Jackie aspired to go into teaching as she saw it as a route
through which she could make a positive social impact, to
'give back' to her community. The motivation to do socially
progressive work has previously been found to play a role in
the career development processes of working-class women
(Silva, 2015). This was a common finding in most of the firmly
working-class women's narratives, and most viewed teaching
as a route through which they could do this work. Many
mentioned that they were keen to work in the 'most disadvantaged' schools. Though they knew this would be challenging, they saw these as sites where they could make the
greatest positive impact. In terms of their prospective career
progression, all wanted to avoid entering management roles as
they believed this would take them out of the classroom. On
this, Jackie said:

> *I teach for the children, for them, to better their
> futures. I'm not there for the money, I don't want to
> go into team leadership. I'll be a class teacher until
> I'm like 78, I don't mind not having a pay cheque
> that's like £60,000 because to me it's for the kids, it's
> not for anything else.*

Further, they perceived management roles as incompatible
with motherhood due to the workload associated with these
positions. Aspirations to become a mother had long been
central to Jackie's crafting of her career goals, she said
'teaching is the thing I wanted to do first, and then I'll become
a mum after that'. The perceived flexibility of being a classroom teacher allowed her to imagine the potential possibility
of both having a career and being a mother.

When considering where she would like to do a PGCE,
she knew she wanted to return home to London and study
at a local university because, as she said, 'I don't want to

stay away from home for any longer than I have to'. Speaking about the prospective impact of moving home, Jackie said:

> It will be like I've never been away, and I'll feel like a child again. Going back home. I still feel really young, and I think that maybe yes I've moved away and been independent but I've always known that I'd be going back home, so it just feels temporary independence. So maybe it'll feel like I haven't graduated at all.

Jackie welcomed being integrated into the family household once again and described this process as an 'easy transition'. After achieving a 2:1, she moved back home and began studying for a PGCE. She had taken all these decisions on her own, to secure a job. This prompted her to reflect on the notion that she had never felt a part of the 'University of Bristol brand', while many graduates who assimilated with this brand were able to use it to find lucrative work:

> I didn't feel I was a typical student at the time and I don't feel like I'm a typical graduate. I don't have contacts, I don't have a job waiting for me at the end of my degree. Some of them were there just for 3 years off before going into work and it doesn't really matter what they got in their degree because at the end of it dad or mum would get them a job doing something somewhere that is well paid.

However, she soon secured a full-time, permanent job teaching in London. As a teacher, Jackie is considered a 'knowledge worker', and she was one of the few working-class women from the *Paired Peers* project who progressed to a 'traditional graduate job'. This role provided her with one of the highest incomes among working-class women, earning £27,000 as a 'newly qualified teacher', which increased to £30,000 a year later. Each year she received a gradual increase in her wages, and seven years after graduating from her PGCE, she reported her salary as between £41,000–50,000. While there is no denying that this is a 'good' graduate wage, in a secure profession, Jackie is 'time poor'. She is contracted to 27.5 hours but works an average of 46, leaving her 'physically and emotionally exhausted' by the workload:

> *There's a high turnover of staff. 10 out of 25 staff have left this year. I think you just can't work there for a long time because you will burn out, you need to do too much, there's too much going on. Everything gets pressured...I've been so stressed and so like upset all the time that if that's what teaching is like I couldn't do it long term.*

Though she anticipated a high workload, and managed this, she did not anticipate that teaching would consume so much of her personal life and take a toll on her mental health:

> *I didn't realize the amount that teachers really do have to put up with, and how emotionally exhausting it can be really. Like you're thinking about these kids all day and you go home and you're dreaming about the kids and the school, you're thinking about school constantly. All you can talk about is school and everyone tells you to shut up!*

Though receiving high wages, she struggled to imagine herself achieving the markers of adulthood that she desired, such as owning a home near her parents and having children, due to insufficient funds and the cost of living in London. When calculating the probability of her being able to move out of the family home, she said that she could not envision being able to afford a deposit for a house within the next five years. Reflecting on this frustrated her, particularly when comparisons were drawn between her achieved milestones and her mother's by age:

> *It makes me really cross. I've worked really hard every day, I paid money to train to be a teacher and I can't even afford to live in the city that I teach in. It's ridiculous. [...] Where I live, I can't afford to move out at the minute. [...] Then Mum doesn't help, she's like 'oh yeah by your age I had two children'. I'm like 'thanks Mum, you really know how to wind me up'.*

Reflecting on her own social mobility, like Adele, Jackie described herself as being in between spaces upon finding work after graduation. She articulated that the social and cultural capital she held and mobilized was 'working-class, completely'. However, she understood that her economic income might be considered middle-class, and she viewed teaching as a 'middle-class profession'. To reconcile these and align herself within a class position, she meditated on:

> *An extra class in between. You know what I mean, like Ofsted when you're good with outstanding features, I guess you're like working-class with middle-class features!*

There is a positive twist to Jackie's story. In 2021, she was still a class teacher, happy at her current school, and had just bought a house with her partner.

SARIAH'S STORY: 'YOUR CLASS CHANGES ONCE YOU GRADUATE'

Sariah is a Black woman from a firmly working-class background: she was raised in London by her mother, a beautician from Nigeria. Describing her mother as being strong, hard-working and 'extremely proud' that Sariah was studying at UWE, she became emotional. Speaking of her mother's aspirations for her and her three siblings, Sariah commented:

> *My Mum didn't go to university but she wants all of her kids to graduate, to be graduates she thinks is very....In my culture, you know, it's important for women especially to be educated.*

She describes herself as always having been 'very driven' to achieve well in education; she frequently attended extracurricular events at school and college to boost her learning. As a teenager she was a self-directed student who looked beyond the curriculum and worked to develop employability skills:

> *I'm quite shy but at college I was encouraged to work with people as a team, because that's an essential skill that you need in employment, you need to be able to communicate with others and teamwork is very important, it's really vital. So through that it really helped me and developed that skill.*

Sariah had aspirations to work in media. She took an A Level in Media Studies but when exploring potential subjects to study at undergraduate level, her father steered her away from this subject and towards Sociology, telling her: 'you must study an academic subject, you must'. While Sariah had considered studying Sociology before, she had reservations:

I thought to myself 'I don't know if I can study something like Sociology or Psychology'…I wasn't very academic. Like I read books but I just wasn't….you know, I never used posh and fancy and sophisticated words, and the background that I'm from as well, like there's not many people that are educated, you know.

When at university, Sariah described herself as a 'lone soldier' and reported often feeling homesick, longing to be at home with her mother where they would watch TV together, cook and go to church on a Sunday. As an undergraduate, she did not develop friendships with students she studied alongside, though she made many attempts. She reported that many of her peers were 'snobby' and treated her as 'inferior':

A lot of people at university think that they're better than everybody. It's like it's a competition, everyone's competing against everyone. Like even though I can relate to other students and we can communicate, I don't think I fit in. I don't think I've ever fitted in.

She was aware from her first term of studying that employers prefer to hire graduates with experience in the industry. Further, she was aware that particular 'soft skills' were considered desirable, such as being perceived as 'competitive', 'go-getters' and 'tough'. These were not attributes that she believed she held and believed she needed to develop these:

The world out there is much more competitive, you have to be really ready for it, so many bold people, bold characters, people who are competitive, who are ambitious, who are go-getters, who are dog-eat-dog sort of people, you just have to be ready for it. You

need more than just your degree, you need to have
the like charisma, you can't be soft. Like I can be soft
at times, I know I have to toughen up, yeah, to be
prepared for what's out there...I'll have to develop
my character, like be strong and be firm.

Sariah sought to craft herself as 'employable' through working hard to curate an attractive CV and gain work experience in relevant industries. However, the only employment contract she was able to secure was low paid and temporary, and this interfered with her studies:

When the workload is so much I can't work, I'm just
working on my assignments, that's the only work
that I'm doing. I can't do paid work. It's hard to do
both.

Though she understood the necessity of gaining contacts within the media industry in order to secure employment post-graduation, Sariah was not able to develop this social capital during her studies. She had aimed to do a work placement during the summer holidays between her second and third year of undergraduate study, but was unable to secure such work.

Sariah graduated with a 2:1 in 2013. She was unable to respond to our messages for four years. In late 2017, she responded to our last call for interviews. She told us that she had been homeless for two years:

I became homeless and I was like sofa-surfing and
sleeping in hostels, in shelters, so I was just basically
for like...it was like basically for like 2 years just
moving from place to place just staying in women's
refuges, in hostels, and just looking for somewhere to
live. Because they couldn't keep me, it was short-term
temporary accommodation, they couldn't keep me

> *there for over like not more than a month so it was*
> *just moving on from place to place. I couldn't work*
> *at the time either because it was so unstable, I didn't*
> *know if I'd be moving to Manchester next or*
> *wherever, it was all over the place.*

She said that the reason she became homeless was due to the cost of studying at university and paying for student accommodation:

> *All my money was going towards my tuition fees and*
> *my accommodation...I didn't save any money and I*
> *wasn't working while I was studying, which I really*
> *wish I had done because I would have had some*
> *savings from working and used that towards getting*
> *a place after university. I didn't plan that well.*

She puts the onus on herself, which is unfair given the financial burden of studying for a degree. Unfortunately, Sariah and her family had grown distant during her studies. Thus, she could not return home after graduation. She said:

> *It was hard because I think really....I wasn't close to*
> *my family at the time so I was on my own really, just*
> *sleeping on the street was hard, a lot of cold nights.*
> *And begging for money as well. And I would look*
> *down on people that do that and be like 'ugh, how*
> *can she beg for money, she's a tramp'. But I was put*
> *in that situation and it wasn't nice but that was the*
> *only way that I could survive at the time, I had to ask*
> *people on the street for money.*

Through a voluntary service she was offered a place in their hostel, and in return she volunteered to work for them. Through this she took part in training programmes and workshops. She was also allocated a support worker who prompted her to get in touch with a local early intervention service in London. When we finally made contact in 2017, she had a safe place to call her own in London. When we offered our condolences for what had happened, she responded: 'It's alright. I survived'.

CONCLUSION

All four young women made attempts to draw on the capital they have within their remit to find secure, professional employment after graduation. However, the opportunities that are available to them are due, in part, to their backgrounds (whether they are firmly-, or upper-, working-class) and the cachet associated with the university through which they obtained their degree. Further, what framed their experiences was the availability to move home, or not. While most were able to use the family home as a safety net, or a stop gap before moving on in their lives, others faced significant hardship without this, as the sad struggles of Sariah show.

7

CONCLUSIONS

The object of this book has been to show how the experiences of HE and subsequent entry into the labour market continue to be shaped by the class and gender of students. The young people from less privileged backgrounds, as others have revealed (Antonucci, 2016; Burke, 2016; Friedman & Lauriston, 2019; Reay et al., 2009), face obstacles in gaining entry to the top-rated graduate jobs. They are likely to earn less, to face greater risk of unemployment and of having to return to the parental home. Despite the fact that young women perform as well as their male peers at university, they still appear to be channelled into jobs traditionally seen as suitable for females, for example, teaching and caring work.

We also wanted to show the mechanisms by which these processes of differentiation are maintained, and the stories told in the previous four chapters exemplify such processes. Middle-class young people are able to use the capitals possessed by their families to negotiate their way through into desirable jobs. They can draw on economic help from their parents to secure accommodation in London, where many of the top graduate jobs are concentrated. They are able to take advantage of unpaid placements and internships, which often lead to permanent employment. Family contacts can help them gain job opportunities; and the cultural capital they accumulated through their upbringing and add to through their extracurricular activities at university enables them to construct impressive CVs. Lacking these capitals, working-class students are at a disadvantage.

Importantly, our research shows that there are major differences within each of the groups we have labelled middle- and working-class. These divisions are commonly described as constituting separate 'class fractions'. Those from the upper ranks of the middle-class have the greatest access to capital resources and use those to move more quickly into highly sought-after occupations, as exemplified by the cases of Hannah and Dylan. Their parents occupy positions in the most prestigious professions, such as law, medicine and academia, or run successful businesses. Young people whose parents work in lower-level professions, such as nursing, teaching or administration, or who hold lower positions in businesses, lack the contacts with powerful sponsors enjoyed by their upper-middle-class peers and have less ample financial support. If their parents have split up and they have been raised within a lone-parent family, they may even be eligible for a student bursary. Their experience, as exemplified by Lauren, may be closer to that of some of the working-class young people.

However, they are still more likely to have cultural assets to draw upon, for example, guidance with applications to university or help with their degree topics, than working-class youths, who, as we have discussed earlier, are not always aware of the 'rules of the game', or, if they are, may not be in a position to play by them. As a result they may experience their university environment like 'a fish out of water' in Bourdieu's phrase (Bourdieu & Wacquant, 1992). For example, Jackie told us how her lecturers at UoB used unfamiliar concepts and references, making her feel excluded.

Despite these disadvantages, working-class graduates often are highly motivated to succeed and have learnt self-reliance in their educational and family lives. For example, they manage money better than their middle-class course mates (Bradley & Ingram, 2012). Those we characterize as upper-working-class may have come from a family where one parent holds a semi-professional job, for example, an electrician father and a nurse mother. They may have slightly more economic capital and strong family support behind them. By contrast, those we label 'firmly-working-class' come from manual family backgrounds (drivers, factory workers, cleaners) where any kind of capitals of value in this context are minimal or lacking. Pioneers, 'strangers in paradise' (Reay et al., 2009), they have to find their own unguided pathway through study and into the labour markets. Unsurprisingly, they have higher rates of drop-out, especially the young men. The women tend to have very strong links with their mothers, which may potentially bring feelings of homesickness, and also induce a strong desire to justify sacrifices made by the family to help them to university.

This emphasis on differences between class fractions is one of the important insights emerging from our study. So, too, is the stress on how class intersects with gender, as shown in the stories of our male and female graduates.

GENDERED CHOICES

When we first asked our participants what they wanted from a career, the males were more likely to talk about money, good prospects and working for a prestigious company, while the women tended to mention working with people or giving something back to the community (Brine & Waller, 2004). In line with this, many young men were drawn towards finance, business and IT, while lots of the young women contemplated teaching or voluntary sector work. Even those women who started off sharing male ambitions to high-status work, such as law, often drifted away, as we saw in the case of Francesca, who was deterred from pursuing a training contract for the bar by the competition. Perhaps the most striking example was Sally, reading Law at UoB, whose case was discussed in our first project book (Bathmaker et al., 2016). Sally told us she wanted to become a 'hotshot lawyer', but changed her mind when observing the long-hours' culture of her parents and their friends. Having a small child, she wanted a better work-life balance, something important to many participants. Sally decided to go into teaching, a job traditionally seen as compatible with mothering because of the shared school holidays. She did, however, retain some of the success orientation of the middle-class, as she told us she thought about becoming a head teacher, or perhaps setting up her own school, a contrast with Jackie, who stated she was not remotely interested in a management role. In 2021, Sally was a sixth form director in an exclusive private school.

By contrast, working-class young women, like Jackie, came to university already set on becoming school teachers. A step up from the manual jobs of their parents, teaching is seen as a secure and reasonably well-rewarded occupation. We have described working-class students as having 'experiential capital', as they come from what used to be called 'the school of hard knocks' or 'university of life'. Often they have seen the realities of poverty and struggle, and it leads them to make sensible, if limited, choices, avoiding the vague upward aspirations of some middle-class women.

Having revealed this persistence of class disadvantage and gender differentiation, which combine to help recreate the social dominance of a white predominantly male elite, we want to emphasize that higher education is still a valuable asset for most who undertake it; perhaps in terms of social mobility the working-class men in Chapter 5 exemplify this best, whilst both the middle-class men and women in Chapters 3 and 4 respectively demonstrate how higher education is used to reproduce social and economic advantage from one generation to another. The graduate premium in lifetime earnings endures, though it has somewhat diminished for many. Graduates are less vulnerable to long-term unemployment (though not immune as the case of Sariah shows). They are more likely in the longer term to acquire secure employment. We can demonstrate this by showing what had happened to some of our graduates 10 years after our study commenced.

WHERE ARE THEY NOW? THE GRADUATES AND THE PANDEMIC

In the autumn of 2021, Jessie Abrahams of Bristol University, a long-term member of the *Paired Peers* team, carried out an online survey of our remaining graduate cohort. She received 36 responses, including many from the graduates featured in this book. The survey sought to explore the graduates' experience of the COVID-19 pandemic and its impact on their working lives, but also collected information on their occupations, their accommodation situation and their personal relationships. What the survey revealed was that those who responded had in the main achieved successful transitions into adulthood. Here we offer a brief summary of some of her key findings.

Of the 56 students who remained at the end of phase two, over half (36) responded to the survey, 21 women and 15 men. In terms of the class we assigned to them at the start of the project, 20 were middle-class and 16, working-class (some of the latter would now be considered upwardly mobile into the middle-class). The smallest category were working-class men: only five responded, including three of those featuring in Chapter 5. This is commonly the hardest group to recruit and retain.

Of the 36, 27 considered themselves in secure or very secure jobs, with only six stating that their position was insecure or very insecure, three from each class. Three were not currently employed, two doing a postgraduate course and the other intending to do so. Given the prevalence of job insecurity, especially during the pandemic, this is a surprising finding, though we may speculate that those who think of themselves as being less successful had not replied to this survey.

In terms of earnings, nine were earning over £50,000 per annum, mainly men, and the majority (14) earned between £31,000 and £50,000. These fairly substantial earnings indicate that the 'graduate premium' is holding up, especially as many of these started on low pay on leaving university, but had achieved promotion or moved into better paid areas. A minority of 10 respondents, however, remained low paid, earning less than £31,000, three of them under £20,000. It is significant that eight of these were women; as we might have predicted, working-class women were the lowest-earning group.

A successful transition to adulthood is seen to encompass not just financial and occupational security, but also starting one's own household and family arrangements. Here again, the graduates had made substantial progress since the end of the project. Given the acknowledged crisis in the housing market, we were startled to find that twenty of them owned a property. It is, of course, easier to do this if there are two earners, and this was largely the case. Twelve of them were married or engaged (one had been married twice!), many were cohabiting with a partner, one was in a 'polyamorous relationship', and only two described themselves as 'single'. Interestingly, there was no difference between the middle- and working-class graduates in terms of property ownership. For example, Ruby, from a working-class background, was once of the most settled, married, in a senior teaching role, with two children, and about to move with her husband into a second house: a fine exemplar of working-class determination and realism.

From the answers about the pandemic's impact on their lives, many had come to value home life more. Sean remarked on the fact that many of his friends had recently decided to marry. Lockdown with its curtailing of social activities seemed to have strengthened relationships and made these young people aware of the importance of the non-work side of life. Most had found themselves working at home, which had produced a degree of stress, but at the same time, it had saved them money formerly spent on travel to work and sustenance, helping them to apply for a mortgage. Thus Francesca, now in a mortgaged property, told us:

> I valued seeing my family a lot more and never thought I'd leave London to move closer to home, but we have decided to do so to be closer to my Mum and Dad. Realized how much I took travelling for granted and cannot wait to do so. But also realized how much travelling for work was stressful (very long days, very early flights and long meetings) which I've been grateful for missing in the last 18 months, conducting them over webex has been a lot more enjoyable.

A number reported how they felt they had become closer to their partners, including Dylan:

Certain aspects have been beneficial (more time with spouse etc.), however of course the normal worries around parents' health etc. Mine and my spouse's lives have remained broadly unchanged apart from more flexible working arrangements. This is a significant improvement given we were commuting to London everyday which takes up a lot of time.

While some graduates did report heightened stress, anxiety and loneliness during lockdowns, even in a couple of cases severe depression, overall the picture from the survey is of resourcefulness in confronting a period of difficulty and taking advantage of the positive aspects offered by the pandemic. We end this section with another positive example of a working-class woman, Bianca, who studied History at UoB. Bianca exemplifies the hard-headed realism mentioned above, describing herself as 'living at home as investment':

When I first graduated I moved home for a couple of years. I then brought my own property and stayed at my parents whilst I renovated it. I then moved out, but moved back home last summer. I currently rent out the property I own and am saving to get a second mortgage.

Bianca runs a property business which covers a range of services (mainly for letting agents) including property inspections and inventory reports. She has one employee. Tutoring in English part-time online contributes to her income in the £51–60,000 band (the highest earnings among the working-class women respondents). She hopes to expand the business, taking more managerial responsibility. Like Jackie, she is a working-class young women with strong attachments to her family, making good use of her HE experience and skills.

WHAT IS TO BE DONE: ADDRESSING INEQUALITIES

In response to the Augur Review on post-18 education and funding, which had recommended lowering fees and reintroducing a small grant, the Conservative Government released a set of policies which worried us greatly. They seem designed to block entry for working-class youth into HE, undoing the achievements of past decades, They included raising entry requirements and requiring higher grades at GCSE in English and maths, traditional areas of weakness for disadvantaged students. Apprentice routes would be pushed for 'less academic' youths. Perhaps most chilling was the proposal to remove widening participation funding from universities whose disadvantaged students don't get high-paid jobs as professionals and managers. As this book has shown, working-class students have to set limited (and realistic) horizons, take longer to earn decent incomes and are more at risk. Nevertheless, over time they achieve economic security, own property and start families; moreover the experience of HE offers new skills, boosts self-confidence and widens perspectives: its benefits should not be reduced to solely measuring economic gains as the government would like to do.

If these proposals are implemented, state schools should perhaps provide remedial teaching in English and maths for disadvantaged students whose parents cannot provide private coaching. This, along with the continued existence of private school is a major factor in recreating class inequality (Reay, 2017). We believe universities should restrict student intake from private schools, aiming towards the national average of 7% attendance at such schools (Sutton Trust, 2019) to make the undergraduate body more representative.

There is much more universities can do. They should provide students with up-to-date information on the state of the graduate labour market, including new areas of work (schools should do this too). They can promote paid work experiences, including funding some themselves as UWE does: they should not advertize unpaid ones or allow businesses who offer them to attend their careers fairs. Most universities now have schemes to promote well-being and tackle mental health problems. The stigma around such problems must be removed, ensuring students feel free to talk about their mental health and seek help early on. Lecturers and tutors, especially those in the elite institutions may need additional training in how to teach inclusively, avoiding patronizing or stereotyping comments, helping working-class to students to feel they 'fit'; after all, they have earned their right to be there.

We believe the government should be pressured to reinstate and increase the Student Finance England grant, which was removed in 2016. Many *Paired Peers* participants received this grant, yet still faced the disadvantage of engaging in term-time employment, as their stories have highlighted. Likewise the Education Maintenance Allowance (EMA) which allowed 16–18 year old students from poorer families to claim financial support for studying, but which was abolished in England shortly after our project began in 2010. With rising fees and rents, plus the current cost-of-living crisis, economic help for those from poorer families is acutely needed.

Governments could do more to open up the labour market. Currently, minimum wage legislation means that unpaid internships are effectively illegal in the UK. However, in 2018 the government failed to prosecute any business on this basis (Butler, 2018): we all know this goes on and it needs to enforce the legislation. It also needs to reinvest in the areas of Britain most affected by austerity policies, promoting HE and FE in these 'left-behind areas' along with job growth. This would enable graduates to resist the pull of London and find secure employment in their home towns, at the same time as regenerating working-class communities. Such moves would be aligned with the Conservative Government's much vaunted 'levelling-up' agenda.

But the main responsibility for improvement lies with employers. They should stop exploiting young adults through unpaid internships, broaden recruitment practices beyond the Russell Group of universities, abandon the stereotypes that lead them only to recruit 'people like us' so that their workforces reflect the diversity of British society. Lengthy recruitment processes, such as those for legal careers, or medicine, could be simplified to make them more accessible to the less wealthy.

Our study has shown that HE does promote social mobility, but only for a few. Rather it frequently helps reproduce social and economic advantage for the already privileged. Based as it is on principles of meritocracy, the ascendance of 'the brightest and best', the social mobility narrative is, we suggest, inadequate and flawed. It needs replacing with a narrative of social justice, even if this means challenging the reproduction of advantage in which universities assist, and trying to tackle the 'glass floor' preventing *downward* social mobility for the sons and daughters of the powerful (Waller, 2011).

END PIECE: SELLING THEIR YOUTH

It's like it's a competition, everyone's competing against everyone.

(Sariah)

We have highlighted in this chapter the successes achieved by many of our participant graduates, some against the odds. Some have been born with the proverbial silver spoon in their mouths; others have had to struggle to overcome obstacles. Luck, determination, hard work, talent and sponsorship have played their part, alongside various capitals, inherited or achieved, including the famous 'bank of mum and dad', in the achievement of secure jobs and adult capacities.

However, we want to emphasize that this has taken place in a hostile environment. The first decades of the twenty-first century are not an easy time to be a young person. While a university degree is an asset, graduates leave burdened with debt and with other people's expectations of what they should achieve. As Sariah indicates, they enter a hypercompetitive labour market, where, as she also says, many players 'are go-getters, who are dog-eat-dog sort of people'. Moreover, the intense competition between companies and employers has impacted extremely adversely on working conditions; work in the 'gig economy', where many graduates start out, is ill-paid and insecure. As firms cut their workforces to increase profits, jobs have been intensified, and increasingly controlled and monitored by technology. As the economy is shaped by the IT giants, such as Amazon, Facebook, Google and Apple, many young workers lead an almost robotic existence (Bradley, 2020; Delfanti, 2021). Only a minority of employees will achieve jobs carrying responsibility and security, and even they are forced to work hours longer than specified in their contracts, as many of the graduates indicated in the survey: Francesca is contracted for 37.5 but works 70.

For many young people, including many of our participants, these conditions have created significant stress and anxiety, contributing to a major epidemic of mental ill-health in the younger age groups. This has been exacerbated by the pandemic, while the pressures on the NHS and social services mean that help for mental problems is limited. Nicholas, who was doing well as an engineer before the pandemic, became depressed and had to take sick leave as a result of work intensification:

> *By the second lockdown, I was overworked due to job cuts at my company, cynical about company attempts to promote 'wellbeing' whilst reducing our*

real-time earnings, and added dark of the wet winter
led to me seeking medical help and being prescribed
anti-depressants.

Lynn, who studied Drama and works for a charity, similarly struggled with the impact of lockdown:

It has been a very real strain. I have pre-existing
mental health conditions which have been
exacerbated. I struggle with feelings of a
misanthropic nature, emptiness, sadness, guilt, anger
on an almost daily basis.

It is interesting that Lynn mentions guilt, given the dominant cultural climate of individualization (Bauman, 1992;
Beck & Beck-Gernsheim, 2001), the viewing of one's life as a
project or task for which we have to take responsibility,
ignoring the context and social structures that surround us. If
life does not turn out a success, we blame ourselves, inducing
feelings of guilt, shame and failure.

These feelings of anxiety arising from individualization and
the pressures of work must be understood in a wider social
and political context. In the UK, the economy struggles from
the combined effects of the COVID pandemic and Brexit. In
the last few years, we have had talk of a housing crisis, a
cost-of-living crisis, an energy crisis and, overarching it, all the
looming climate crisis. The gap between the rich and the poor
has widened, society is further polarizing economically and
socially, political differences have magnified and the world is
increasingly divided and riven with wars. Membership of the
EU opened up employment chances overseas for graduates
such as Adrian in Chapter 3 which are now closing off. No
wonder young adults increasingly suffer from anxiety! It is in
this climate that they must survive by 'selling their youth' in a
savage and unforgiving market.

Many of us who are older and more settled have buffers against these crises: savings, mortgages, property and pensions. The young, however, are the future of our country and our world. It is up to us to take care of them, to listen to their concerns, try to respond to their demands and support political campaigns to make their lives better. The responsibility for their well-being falls upon us all, and not simply them as individuals.

REFERENCES

Abrahams, J. (2017). Honourable mobility or shameless entitlement? Habitus and graduate employment. *British Journal of Sociology of Education, 38*(5), 625–640.

Antonucci, L. (2016). *Student lives in crisis*. The Policy Press.

Ashton, D., & Field, D. (1975). *Young workers: From school to work*. Hutchinson.

Atkinson, W. (2010). *Class, individualization and late modernity*. Palgrave.

Bathmaker, A.-M., Ingram, N., Abrahams, J., Hoare, T., Waller, R., & Bradley, H. (2016). *Higher education, social class and social mobility*. Palgrave.

Bathmaker, A.-M., Ingram, N., & Waller, R. (2013). Higher education, social class and the mobilisation of capitals: Recognising and playing the game. *British Journal of Sociology of Education, 34*(5/6), 723–743.

Bauman, Z. (1992). *Intimations of postmodernism*. Routledge.

Beck, U., & Beck-Gernsheim, E. (2001). *Individualization: Institutionalized individualism and its social and political consequences*. Sage.

Blanchflower, D. (2019). *Not working: Where have all the good jobs gone*. Oxford University Press.

Bourdieu, P., & Wacquant, L. (1992). *An invitation to reflexive sociology*. University of Chicago Press.

Bradley, H. (1989). *Men's work, women's work*. Polity.

Bradley, H. (2016). *Fractured identities: Changing patterns of inequality* (2nd ed.). Polity.

Bradley, H. (2017). Should I stay or should I go? Dilemmas and decisions among UK undergraduates. *European Journal of Educational Research*, *16*(1), 30–44.

Bradley, H. (2020). Crisis at work: Gender, class and the dehumanisation of jobs. *Historical Studies in Industrial Relations*, *41*(5), 111–137.

Bradley, H., & Devadason, R. (2008). Fractured transitions: Young adults' pathways into contemporary labour markets. *Sociology*, *48*(3), 119–136.

Bradley, H., Healy, G., Forson, C., & Kaul, P. (2007). Ethnic minority women and workplace cultures: What works and what doesn't. Report to EOC.

Bradley, H., & Ingram, N. (2012). Banking on the future: Choices, aspirations and economic hardship in working-class student experience. In W. Atkinson, S. Roberts, & M. Savage (Eds.), *Class inequality in austerity Britain* (pp. 51–69). Palgrave Macmillan.

Bradley, H., & Van Hoof, J. (Eds.). (2005). *Young people in Europe*. The Policy Press.

Brine, J., & Waller, R. (2004). Working-class women on an access course: Risk, opportunity and (re)constructing identities. *Gender and Education*, *16*(1), 97–113.

Brown, P., Lauder, H., & Ashton, D. (2011). *The global auction, the broken promises of education, jobs and incomes*. Oxford University Press.

Brown, P., & Tannock, S. (2009). Education, meritocracy and the global war for talent. *Journal of Education Policy, 24,* 377–392.

Burke, C. (2016). *Culture, capitals and graduate futures: Degrees of class.* Taylor & Francis.

Butler, S. (2018). Initiative to crack down on unpaid internships launched by UK. *The Guardian.* February 8.

Charlesworth, S. (2000). *A phenomenology of working class experience.* Cambridge University Press.

Coles, B. (1995). *Youth and social policy: Youth, citizenship and young careers.* UCL Press.

Czarniawska, B. (2004). *Narratives in social science research.* Sage.

Dale, A., & Shaheen, N. (1999). Routes into education and employment for young Pakistani and Bangladeshi women. Paper presented at University of Manchester.

Delfanti, A. (2021). *The warehouse: Workers and robots at Amazon.* Pluto Press.

Department for Education. (2010). Schools, pupils and their characteristics, January 2010. https://assets.publishing.service. gov.uk/government/uploads/system/uploads/attachment_data/ file/218952/main_20text_20sfr092010.pdf

Devine, F. (2004). *Class practices: How parents help their children get good jobs.* Cambridge University Press.

Edmiston, D., Baumberg Geiger, B., De Vries, R., Scullion, L., Summers, K., Ingold, J., Robertshaw, D., Gibbons, A., & Karagiannaki, E. (2020). Who are the new COVID-19 cohort of benefit claimants? http://hub.salford.ac.uk/welfare-at-a-social-distance/wp-content/uploads/sites/120/2020/09/WaSD-Rapid-Report-2-New-COVID-19-claimants.pdf

Elias, P., & Purcell, K. (2013). *Classifying graduate occupations for the knowledge society*. Institute for Employment Research, University of Warwick.

Enneli, P., Modood, T., & Bradley, H. (2002). *Young Turks: A set of 'invisible' disadvantaged groups*. Report to Joseph Rowntree Foundation.

Erikson, R., & Goldthorpe, J. (1992). *The constant flux: A study of class mobility in industrial societies*. Clarendon Press.

Evans, S. (2010). Becoming 'somebody': Examining class and gender through higher education. In Y. Taylor (Ed.), *Classed intersections: Spaces, selves, knowledge*. Ashgate.

Frazier, E. F. (1965). *Black bourgeoisie: Rise of a new middle-class*. Free Press.

Freie, C. (2010). Considering gendered careers: The influence of resilient mothers and sisters upon white working-class young women. *Ethnography and Education, 5*(3), 229–243.

Friedman, S., & Lauriston, D. (2019). *The class ceiling: Why it pays to be privileged*. Policy Press.

Furlong, A., & Cartmel, F. (2007). *Young people and social change*. Open University Press.

Graham, L. O. (2000). *Our kind of people: Inside America's black upper class*. Harper Collins.

Green, F., & Kynaston, D. (2019). *Engines of Privilege: Britain's private school problem*. Bloomsbury.

Gunter, A., & Watt, P. (2009). Grafting, going to college and working on road; youth transitions and cultures in an East London neighbourhood. *Journal of Youth Studies, 12*(5), 515–529.

High Fliers. (2018). *The Graduate Market in 2018; annual review of graduate vacancies & starting salaries at the UK's leading employers*. High Fliers.

Higher Education Statistics Association (HESA). (2012). Students in higher education 2010/11. https://www.hesa.ac.uk/data-and-analysis/publications/students-2010-11

Hoare, A., & Corver, M. (2010). The regional geography of new young graduate labour in the UK. *Regional Studies*, *44*(4), 477–494.

Hollands, R. (1997). *The long transition: Class, culture and youth training*. Macmillan.

Howker, E., & Malik, S. (2013). *Jilted Generation; how Britain has bankrupted its youth*. Icon Books.

Ingram, N., Abrahams, J., Bathmaker, A.-M., Bentley, L., Bradley, H., Hoare, A. H., Papafilippou, V., & Waller, R. (forthcoming). *The degree generation: Moving on up in the graduate labour market?* The Policy Press.

Ingram, N., & Waller, R. (2014). Working- and middle-class male undergraduates constructions of contemporary masculine identities. In S. Roberts (Ed.), *Debating modern masculinities: Change, continuity, crisis?* Palgrave Macmillan.

Ingram, N., & Waller, R. (2015). Higher education and the reproduction of social elites. *Discover Society*, *20*. http://www.discoversociety.org/2015/05/05/higher-education-and-the-reproduction-of-social-elites/

Joliffe, P., & Collins, H. (2019). *Warnings of a 'race to the bottom' on workers' pay and conditions should concern us all*. The Conversation. November 27.

Jones, G. (2005). Social protection policies for young people; a cross-national perspective. In H. Bradley & J. Van Hoof (Eds.), *Young people in Europe*. The Policy Press.

Jones, O. (2011). *Chavs: The demonization of the working class*. Verso.

Jones, O. (2014). *The establishment: And how they get away with it*. Penguin.

Kelly, L. (2020). Young talented and jobless. *The Sunday Times*. November 22.

Koch, L., Fransham, M., Cant, S., Ebrey, J., Glucksberg, L., & Savage, M. (2021). Social polarisation at the local level: A four-town comparative study on the challenges of politicising inequality in Britain. *Sociology*, *55*(1), 3–29.

Lareau, A. (2003). *Unequal childhoods class, race and family life*. University of California Press.

Lawler, S. (1999). 'Getting out and getting away': women's narratives of class mobility. *Feminist Review*, *63*(1), 3–24.

MacDonald, R., Shildrick, T., & Furlong, A. (2020). 'Cycles of disadvantage' revisited: Young people, families and poverty across generations. *Journal of Youth Studies*, *23*(1), 12–27.

McDonald, R. (2005). *Disconnected youth? Growing up in Britain's poor neighbourhoods*. Palgrave.

McDowell, L. (1996). *Capital culture*. Blackwell.

McDowell, L. (2003). *Redundant masculinities: White working-class youth and employment*. Blackwell.

McInnes, J. (1998). *The end of masculinity*. Open University Press.

McRobbie, A. (2008). *The aftermath of feminism*. Sage.

Morrison, A. (2014). 'You have to be well spoken': Students' views on employability within the graduate labour market. *Journal of Education and Work*, 27(2), 179–198.

Murray, C. (1990). *The emerging British underclass*. Institute of Economic Affairs.

Murray, C. (1994). *Underclass: The crisis deepens*. Institute of Economic Affairs.

ONS. (2019). https://www.nisra.gov.uk/statistics/labour-market-and-social-welfare/labour-force-survey

Papafilippou, V., & Bentley, L. (2017). Gendered transitions, career identities and possible selves: The case of engineering graduates. *Journal of Education and Work*, 30(8), 827–839.

Plummer, K. (1994). *Telling sexual stories*. Routledge.

Plummer, K. (2019). *Narrative power: The struggle for humanity*. Polity.

Prince's Trust Mosaic. (2021). mosaicnetwork.co.uk

Purcell, K., Elias, P., Atfield, G., Behle, H., Ellison, R., & Luchinskaya, D. (2013). *Transitions into employment, further study and other outcomes: The futuretrack stage 4 report*. Warwick: Higher Education Careers Services Unit.

Putnam, R. (2000). *Bowling alone: The collapse and revival of American community*. Simon & Schuster.

Reay, D. (2017). *Miseducation: Inequality, education and the working-class*. The Policy Press.

Reay, D., Crozier, G., & Clayton, J. (2009). 'Strangers in paradise?' Working-class students in elite universities. *Sociology*, 43(6), 1103–1121.

Roberts, K. (1995). *Youth and employment in modern Britain*. University Press.

Sennett, R., & Cobb, J. (1977). *The hidden injuries of class*. University Press.

Silva, J. (2015). *Coming up short: Working-class adulthood in an age of uncertainty*. Oxford University Press.

Skeggs, B. (1997). *Formations of class and gender: Becoming respectable*. Sage.

Social Mobility Commission. (2019). *State of the Nation 2018–2019. Social mobility in Great Britain*. Social Mobility Commission.

Sparkes, A. (2003). Editorial. *Auto/Biography, XI*, 1–2.

Standing, G. (2011). *The precariat: The new dangerous class*. Bloomsbury.

Sutton Trust. (2019). *Elitist Britain 2019: The educational backgrounds of Britain's leading people*. Sutton Trust.

Toft, M., & Friedman, S. (2021). The family, wealth and the class ceiling: The propulsive power of the bank of mum and dad. *Sociology, 55*(1), 90–109.

UCAS. (2021). Record levels of young people accepted into university. https://www.ucas.com/corporate/news-and-key-documents/news/record-levels-young-people-accepted-university

Walkerdine, V., & Lucey, H. (1989). *Democracy in the kitchen: Regulating mothers and socializing daughters*. Virago.

Waller, R. (2011). The sociology of education. In B. Dufour & W. Curtis (Eds.), *Studying education: Key disciplines in education studies* (pp. 106–131). Open University Press.

Waller, R., Hodge, S., Holford, J., Milana, M., & Webb, S. (2018). Adult education, mental health and mental wellbeing. *International Journal of Lifelong Education, 37*(4), 397–400.

Weekes-Barnard, D. (2018). *Integration strategy must focus on tackling poverty for BME families*. Joseph Rowntree Foundation, Blog. June 8.

Wenham, A. (2020). 'Wish you were here?' geographies of exclusion: Young people, coastal towns and marginality. *Journal of Youth Studies, 23*(1), 44–60.

Willetts, D. (2010). *The pinch: How the baby boomers took their children's future and why they should give it back*. Atlantic Books.

Willis, P. (1977). *Learning to labour: How working-class kids get working-class jobs*. Saxon House.

INDEX